Table of Contents – Reality Factory 3D Game Creation 2015 (Vol. 1)

License Agreement

This book (the "Book") is a product provided by HobbyPRESS (being referred to as "HobbyPRESS" in this document), subject to your compliance with the terms and conditions set forth below. PLEASE READ THIS DOCUMENT CAREFULLY BEFORE ACCESSING OR USING THE BOOK. BY ACCESSING OR USING THE BOOK, YOU AGREE TO BE BOUND BY THE TERMS AND CONDITIONS SET FORTH BELOW. IF YOU DO NOT WISH TO BE BOUND BY THESE TERMS AND CONDITIONS, YOU MAY NOT ACCESS OR USE THE BOOK. HOBBYPRESS MAY MODIFY THIS AGREEMENT AT ANY TIME, AND SUCH MODIFICATIONS SHALL BE EFFECTIVE IMMEDIATELY UPON POSTING OF THE MODIFIED AGREEMENT ON THE CORPORATE SITE OF HOBBYPRESS. YOU AGREE TO REVIEW THE AGREEMENT PERIODICALLY TO BE AWARE OF SUCH MODIFICATIONS AND YOUR CONTINUED ACCESS OR USE OF THE BOOK SHALL BE DEEMED YOUR CONCLUSIVE ACCEPTANCE OF THE MODIFIED AGREEMENT.

Restrictions on Alteration
You may not modify the Book or create any derivative work of the Book or its accompanying documentation. Derivative works include but are not limited to translations.

Restrictions on Copying
You may not copy any part of the Book unless formal written authorization is obtained from us.

LIMITATION OF LIABILITY

HobbyPRESS will not be held liable for any advice or suggestions given in this book. If the reader wants to follow a suggestion, it is at his or her own discretion. Suggestions are only offered to help.

IN NO EVENT WILL HOBBYPRESS BE LIABLE FOR (I) ANY INCIDENTAL, CONSEQUENTIAL, OR INDIRECT DAMAGES (INCLUDING, BUT NOT LIMITED TO, DAMAGES FOR LOSS OF PROFITS, BUSINESS INTERRUPTION, LOSS OF PROGRAMS OR INFORMATION, AND THE LIKE) ARISING OUT OF THE USE OF OR INABILITY TO USE THE BOOK. EVEN IF HOBBYPRESS OR ITS AUTHORIZED REPRESENTATIVES HAVE BEEN ADVISED OF THE POSSIBILITY OF SUCH DAMAGES, OR (II) ANY CLAIM ATTRIBUTABLE TO ERRORS, OMISSIONS, OR OTHER INACCURACIES IN THE BOOK.

You agree to indemnify, defend and hold harmless HobbyPRESS, its officers, directors, employees, agents, licensors, suppliers and any third party information providers to the Book from and against all losses, expenses, damages and costs, including reasonable attorneys' fees, resulting from any violation of this Agreement (including negligent or wrongful conduct) by you or any other person using the Book.

Miscellaneous.

This Agreement shall all be governed and construed in accordance with the laws of Hong Kong applicable to agreements made and to be performed in Hong Kong. You agree that any legal action or proceeding between

HobbyPRESS and you for any purpose concerning this Agreement or the parties' obligations hereunder shall be brought exclusively in a court of competent jurisdiction sitting in Hong Kong.

Preface

The RF software had revolutionized the world of Windows based 3D game creation, by providing easy drag-and-drop kind of interface for producing complex game logic and physics, with the additional capability of importing custom textures and models, and producing special effects through modern 3D chipset's features.

This is not a step-by-step tutorial. This is also not a guide book kind of overview material. We place our focus on the practical side of game creation - practical tips and techniques one will definitely need when starting out a 3D game project. We also tell exactly what can and cannot be done with RF, and the kind of performance drawback that can be foreseen when the platform is not fed with the right inputs.

So, are you ready for the challenge?

Version Information

The screen captures presented in this book are based on version 0.76 of RF (Reality Factory). Concepts and techniques do apply to all other versions. Note that the software is available FREE OF CHARGE by web download as of the time of this writing – there is no disc version being offered.

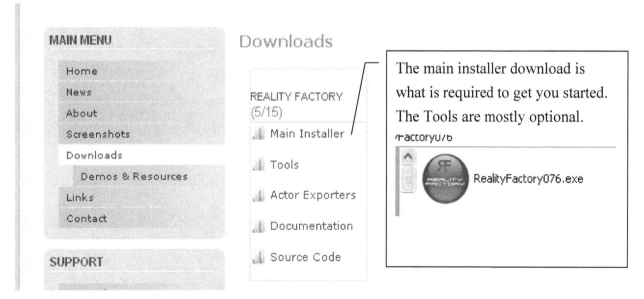

The main installer download is what is required to get you started. The Tools are mostly optional.

The main installer comes with a full set of tools ready for use. Additional tools are available when you browse the tools folder.

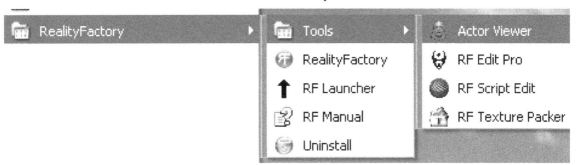

As of the time of this writing there is a pre release download of version 0.78. This version is not yet recommended for production use though.

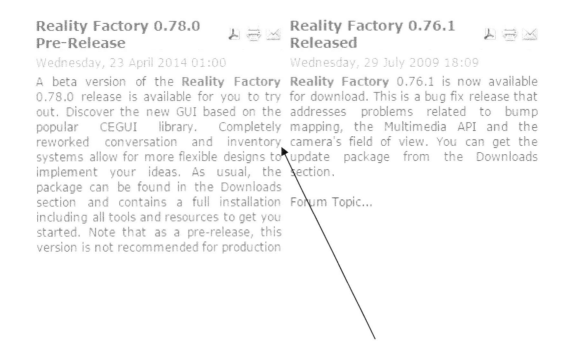

Reality Factory 0.78.0 Pre-Release

Wednesday, 23 April 2014 01:00

A beta version of the **Reality Factory** 0.78.0 release is available for you to try out. Discover the new GUI based on the popular CEGUI library. Completely reworked conversation and inventory systems allow for more flexible designs to implement your ideas. As usual, the package can be found in the Downloads section and contains a full installation including all tools and resources to get you started. Note that as a pre-release, this version is not recommended for production

Reality Factory 0.76.1 Released

Wednesday, 29 July 2009 18:09

Reality Factory 0.76.1 is now available for download. This is a bug fix release that addresses problems related to bump mapping, the Multimedia API and the camera's field of view. You can get the update package from the Downloads section.

Forum Topic...

Basic Concepts

What is a 3D Game Engine?

A game engine is a high level software which provides all the facilities and services a 3D game would need to run, including a 3D engine, a sound engine, a network engine, a physics engine, an Input/Output engine, and possibly an Artificial Intelligence (AI) engine. A 3D engine is meant to render 3D images on a screen. It makes use of a low level Application Programming Interface (API) to communicate to the hardware through the proper display driver. *RF is a game development shell which includes a third party 3D engine and other necessary engines. It also provides an user interface in the form of a visual editor so you can integrate game objects visually for building a complete virtual world without coding.*

The third party 3D engine behind RF is Genesis 3D.

You do NOT need to separately download Genesis3D to get RF to work.

What kinds of game is RF optimized for?

RF can be used to create a wide range of windows based 3D games. However, as a shell, RF is most commonly used for creating action shooter (1st person and 3rd person).

RF provides you with several default players, weapons, camera views and "dashboard" so as soon as you have your level ready you can get the game up and running.

The system is based on an object oriented architecture. The drag and drop interface makes it possible for beginners to "write" simple 3D game programs by putting objects together visually.

Can I use RF to create commercial quality 3D games?

A commercial quality game requires commercial quality graphics, models, sounds, music, and many other factors. RF is capable of putting these media contents together for forming a high quality game. However, you must prepare these contents yourself. Also, RF comes with a demo game which is supposed to act as a template for you to further modify. In a sense you are bound to this template.

Why should we care about physics? Is Physics supported?

Physics allow models to behave like the real stuff. Gravity is an example. The Genesis 3D engine supports physics. However, to fine tune and further customize the physical behavior of special object type, coding beyond RF will be required.

Is RF 2D capable?

The Genesis3D engine is 3D only. If you need to create 2D games, go for Multimedia Fusion 2 (MMF2) or Game Maker 8 (GM8).

Is RF capable of creating FPS game?

Yes. In fact both 1st-person and 3rd-person view modes are supported. The view modes are already preset so you do not need to make explicit arrangement for them to work. At the time you compile a game there is a Preview option. Use that option and the game can start with the default 1st person view mode. Pressing F2 and F3 can switch to other modes on the fly.

Is RF capable of creating 3D game run under a bird eye view?

Sure. RF can be used to create action shooter from a $1^{st}/3^{rd}$ person perspective as well as from sort of a bird eye view. During the game you can press F1, F2 or F3 to switch between modes.

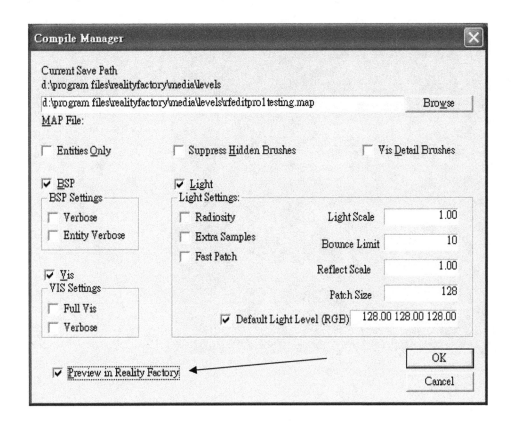

The default mode (F1):

F2:

F3:

There is no need for you to setup any chasing camera.

How do I activate my copy of RF? How do I update, extend and/or

patch the RF program?

We do not find any explicit activation procedure along the process of installing and operating RF.

You need to visit the official RF web site and download fixes and patches. As of the time of this writing the URL is: http://www.realityfactory.info/cms/

Can I sell the game I create through RF?

Yes you can. The license that comes with RF does not restrict you from selling your creation. When redistributing your game, however, you want to know the following terms related to the Genesis3D engine:

The Genesis3D License is an Open Source license with the following main requirements:
- *You must release any code modifications to the engine or any of the accompanying tools*
- *You must display the Genesis3D logo as the first logo of the game*
- *The logo cannot be modified or removed*

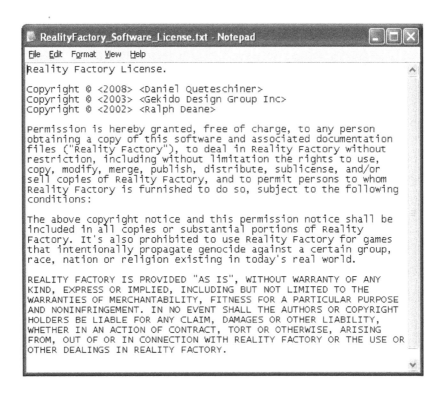

If my game uses those stock 3D models included in the RF

package, do I need to pay a license fee?

Not likely. However, without your own 3D contents your game may be very difficult to sell.

Can I establish copyright on the game I create through RF?

Yes of course. Do make sure you use 3D models and artworks/sound effects that you create on your own or those that are royalty free.

If you use contents that are not royalty free, you will need to make payment arrangement with the source.

What is the difference between Direct3D and OpenGL? Which one

of them is required for running RF?

They are the mainstream 3D APIs currently available. They both provide an interface to the same underlying hardware. They do differ in quality and implementations.

Generally speaking, 3D gaming would use Direct3D (D3D),

while professional 3D modeling would use OpenGL. Most modern display cards found in PC desktops are for sure D3D compatible.

RF supports both. However, for the gaming market you should opt for D3D support.

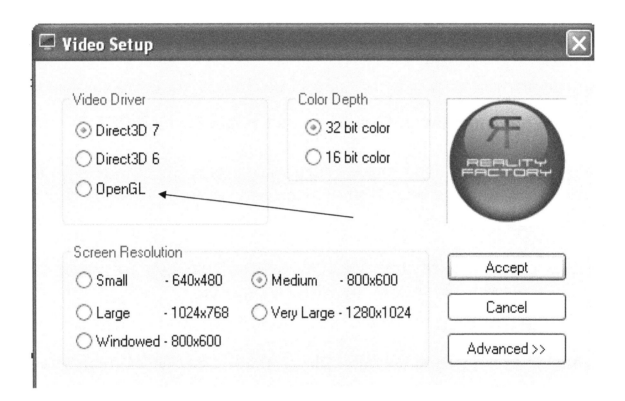

Which DirectX version should I have on my development station?

D3D is part of DirectX. We recommend that you have the latest version to ensure proper program launch.

DirectX consists of the following display related components:

- DirectDraw
- Direct3D

DirectDraw provides video memory management and hardware-accelerated blitting and page flipping capabilities. It is most useful for creating full screen programs as it can define both the screen resolution and color depth programmatically for you. Direct3D works with DirectDraw for providing hardware acceleration for 3D operations.

DirectX drivers can be accessed through MS web site: http://www.microsoft.com/games/en-US/aboutGFW/pages/directx.aspx

Note that for RF to run, you only need the end user runtime.

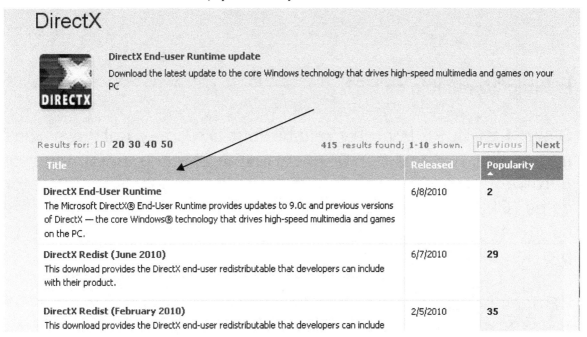

Copyright 2015. **The HobbyPRESS (Hong Kong)**. All rights reserved.

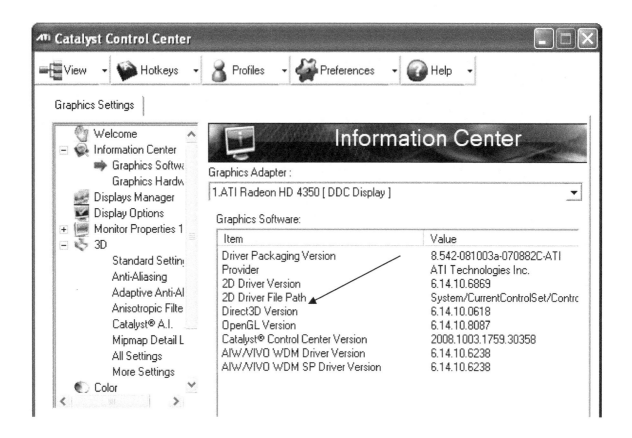

Is Direct3D reliable on RF?

Okay, I think RF is pretty reliable but D3D may not be perfect across all systems. D3D allows you to take advantage of hardware rendering and blitting using graphics accelerator chips (GPU) on the modern video cards. The thing is, there are so many different chips out there, it is just impossible to provide all of them with perfect support.

RF does not access the hardware directly. It goes through D3D. If D3D does not work well on a piece of hardware, don't expect anything better from RF.

A lot of the time the problem is not from the hardware but the driver. If your hardware is from a name brand source, you will likely have a better driver.

RF makes use of a log file for recording D3D related events:

```
D3DDrv.Log - Notepad
File  Edit  Format  View  Help

EnumTextureFormatsCallback: 32, A:ff000000, R:ff0000, G:ff00, B:ff / 32,
U:ff0000, V:ff00, L:ff / 4CC:0 Texture Support Found
EnumTextureFormatsCallback: 8, A:0, R:ff, G:0, B:0 / 8, U:ff, V:0, L:0 / 4CC:0
Texture Support Found
EnumTextureFormatsCallback: 0, A:0, R:0, G:0, B:0 / 0, U:0, V:0, L:0 /
4CC:31545844 Texture Support Found
EnumTextureFormatsCallback: 0, A:0, R:0, G:0, B:0 / 0, U:0, V:0, L:0 /
4CC:32545844 Texture Support Found
EnumTextureFormatsCallback: 0, A:0, R:0, G:0, B:0 / 0, U:0, V:0, L:0 /
4CC:33545844 Texture Support Found
EnumTextureFormatsCallback: 0, A:0, R:0, G:0, B:0 / 0, U:0, V:0, L:0 /
4CC:34545844 Texture Support Found
EnumTextureFormatsCallback: 0, A:0, R:0, G:0, B:0 / 0, U:0, V:0, L:0 /
4CC:35545844 Texture Support Found
EnumTextureFormatsCallback: 8, A:ff, R:0, G:0, B:0 / 8, U:0, V:0, L:0 / 4CC:0
Texture Support Found
EnumTextureFormatsCallback: 8, A:f0, R:f, G:0, B:0 / 8, U:f, V:0, L:0 / 4CC:0
Texture Support Found
EnumSurfaceFormatsCallback: 32, A:0, R:8, G:ffffff, B:ff000000 Texture Support
Found
EnumSurfaceFormatsCallback: 32, A:0, R:8, G:ffffff, B:ff000000 Texture Support
Found
EnumSurfaceFormatsCallback: 32, A:0, R:ff0000, G:ff00, B:ff Texture Support Found
EnumSurfaceFormatsCallback: 32, A:0, R:ff0000, G:ff00, B:ff Texture Support Found
D3DMain_GetSurfaceFormats:   Unable to find a 888 (24-bit) texture support.
D3DMain_GetSurfaceFormats:   Unable to find 556 (16-bit) bump map support.
D3DMain_GetSurfaceFormats:   Unable to find 888 (24-bit) bump map support.
--- D3DMain_SetRenderState ---
--- D3DMain_GetTextureMemory ---
  Ram free: 1047191520

 ** Initialization was successful **

THandle_CheckCache:  Resetting texture cache...
   NO 3dfx card detected, using larger number of handles...
THandle_CheckCache:  Resetting texture cache...
   NO 3dfx card detected, using larger number of handles...
THandle_CheckCache:  Resetting texture cache...
   NO 3dfx card detected, using larger number of handles...

--- D3DMain_ShutdownD3D ---
  Shutdown was successful...
```

If you need further information on D3D, visit Microsoft's Developer Network (MSDN) web site.

Why is RF a good choice for elementary game creation? RF as a shell – what does it mean?

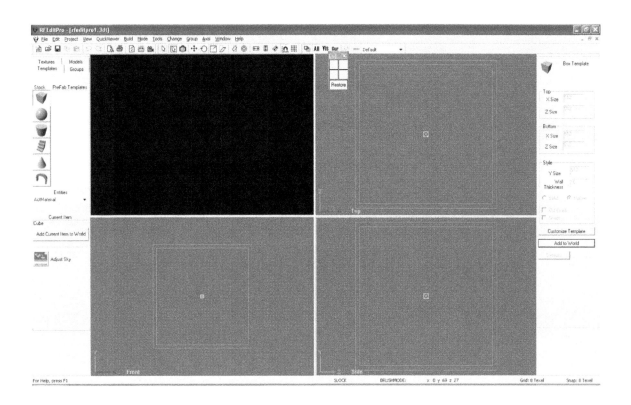

RF is a shell for the more complicated Genesis3D engine. Genesis3D is more for serious coders with richer technical backgrounds. RF aims to reduce the complexity involved in using Genesis3D for game building b acting as a user friendly middleman.

With the editor UI provided by RF, you can pick the desired objects and drag/drop them together, then let RF handle the background stuff (such as program logic, collision detection ...etc) for you.

The best thing about RF is that you can really put together a basic 3D game without coding. This factor alone makes RF a good choice for rapid game prototyping.

Why should one prefer RF over other development platforms for

3D game creation?

RF offers a lot of functionalities without charging you a penny. It is free of charge, and the license has no restrictive terms (in terms of selling your creation) at all.

Some people complain that RF runs quite slow as a game engine. This is a topic heavily debated on the web. I personally think the runtime performance of RF created games is not bad at all.

How does RF compare to The Game Maker 8 (GM8) in terms of 3D

game creation?

RF was born to be 3D. GM8 is 2D (and will always be 2D), with very few native 3D functions. There are third party 3D extensions for GM8, and almost all of them would require significant amount of coding.

Since GM8's 3D functions allow (and often require) coding, room for customization is abundant. However, runtime performance is not that satisfactory. After all, GM8 was not designed with real serious 3D in mind.

How does RF compare to The 3D GameMaker (T3DGM) in terms of

3D game creation?

T3DGM is kind of template based – you create games using ready made building block of all kinds. Since coding is not allowed, room for flexibility is relatively limited. Also, resolution is fixed at 800 x 600 and there is not much you can change in terms of display configuration.

RF allows you to fine tune many properties of the game objects. Display settings can be fully customized as well.

T3DGM's license prohibits profit making. RF does not have such restriction.

How does RF compare to FPS Creator in terms of 3D game

creation?

FPS Creator is for creating first person shooter only. RF can be used to create a wide range of 3D games, with first person view and third person view (plus bird eye view) fully supported.

For beginners, I can tell you that RF is more difficult to use then the FPS Creator. The editing interface is more complicated, and there are way less ready made components (model packs) you can use to quickly put together a game. Also, setting up the various RF tools would require manual configuration of some ini files to avoid errors. Installation of FPS Creator is relatively easy.

How does RF compare to 3DRAD in terms of 3D game creation?

3DRAD has rich support for vehicle dynamics. If you are creating a car racing game, 3DRAD may be a better choice.

RF's editor combines level design and model design together. You can actually design the models directly through the editor without using other third party tools. 3DRAD's editor is for level design only – to make and edit models you need tools from somewhere else.

Is RF a good choice for advanced level game creation?

Based on my experience with the RF UI and the actual performance outcome, I am comfortable to tell you that RF is capable of creating professional 3D game prototypes.

Can I use RF to create WEB games? Are the games Java/Flash

compatible?

RF produces local Win32 executables. It does not produce Java applets nor Flash movies.

Is RF going to be easy if I have rich background in procedural

programming languages?

Put it this way, creating a good game may require good logical thinking skills. Therefore, what you have learnt from your programming experience may be helpful (you will likely have very clear and accurate logic flow).

Can I master RF without understanding any programming concept?

Yes. Even though RF works as a visual tool, its core is no different from a traditional object oriented (OO) development system. It is fully event driven internally. The development environment has the technical details totally hidden so you don't need to know the programming stuff involved.

However, if you want to progress into a more advanced level, you should get yourself truly familiar with the OO concepts. Keep in mind, at the end of the day all 3D games are OO based.

What is the function of the RF Editor? How does it work?

There are several different level editors available for RF. The one that comes with the main installer is located in the tools folder. It is called RFEDITPRO.

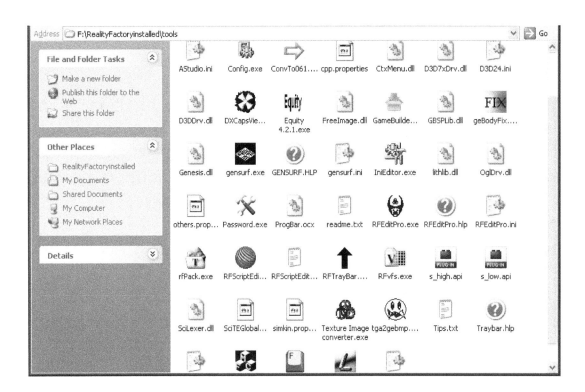

Address [F:\RealityFactoryinstalled\tools] Go

File and Folder Tasks
- Make a new folder
- Publish this folder to the Web
- Share this folder

Other Places
- RealityFactoryinstalled
- My Documents
- Shared Documents
- My Computer
- My Network Places

Details

AStudio.ini	Config.exe	ConvTo061....	cpp.properties	CtxMenu.dll	D3D7xDrv.dll	D3D24.ini
D3DDrv.dll	DXCapsVie...	Equity 4.2.1.exe	FreeImage.dll	GameBuilde...	GBSPLib.dll	geBodyFix....
Genesis.dll	gensurf.exe	GENSURF.HLP	gensurf.ini	IniEditor.exe	lithlib.dll	OglDrv.dll
others.prop...	Password.exe	ProgBar.ocx	readme.txt	RFEditPro.exe	RFEditPro.hlp	RFEditPro.ini
rfPack.exe	RFScriptEdi...	RFScriptEdit...	RFTrayBar....	RFvfs.exe	s_high.api	s_low.api
SciLexer.dll	SciTEGlobal...	simkin.prop...	Texture Image converter.exe	tga2gebmp....	Tips.txt	Traybar.hlp

RFEditPro.exe　　RFEditPro.hlp　　RFEditPro.ini

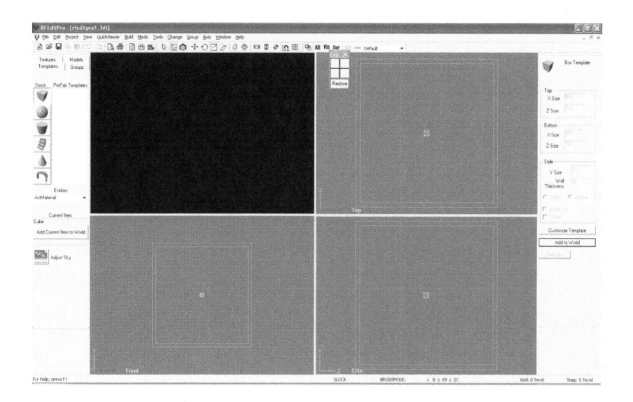

From RF's web site you can download two different alternative editors. One is called RfEdit. Another is called the Genesis World Editor.

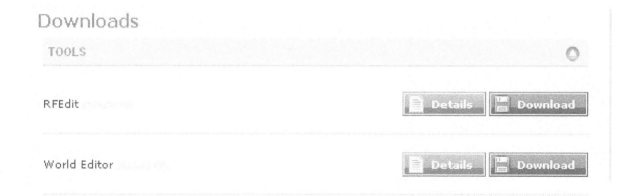

These two editors are very similar in layout and functionality.

RFEdit:

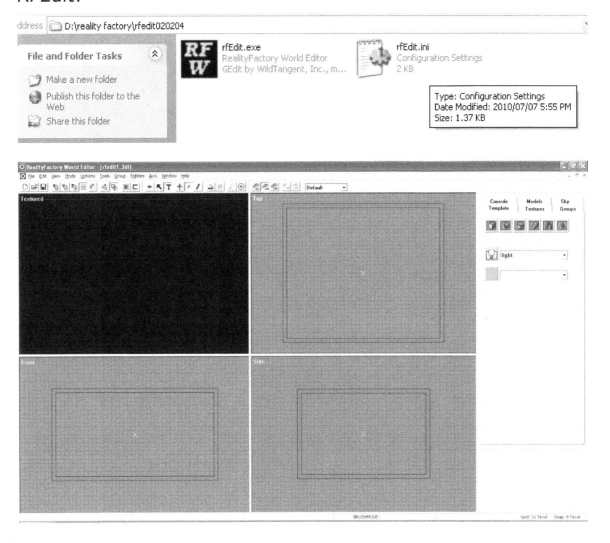

Genesis3D World Editor:

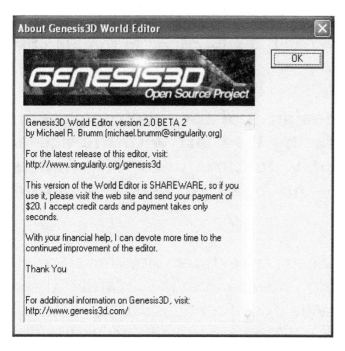

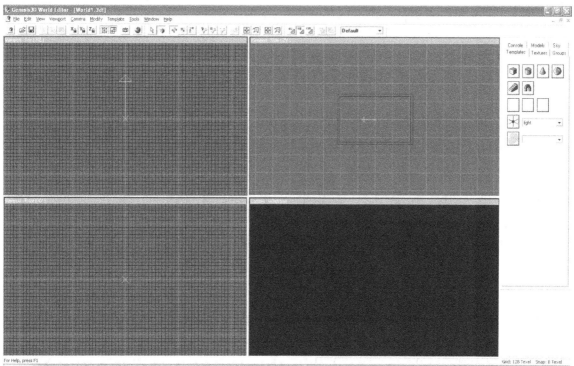

These editors achieve similar purpose – they let you edit the level and the stuff within the level. As described in the help file of one of them:

The editor serves as a design tool for level designers, and as a place for interfacing level art with the actual application (you can apply texture onto 3D models directly via the editor – no need to use a separate texture mapping tool).

All these editors have four Views: a Textured view for showing a 3-dimensional rendering level preview, and three orthographic views that provide Top, Front, and Side views of your level. You do all of your 3D geometry editing within the three orthographic views.

What is special about an event driven system? How does it work?

In an event driven environment, a program is structured in terms of events, with no preordered flow of control. Things do NOT start and proceed step by step. Instead, actions are associated with events, which will get invoked only when the corresponding event conditions are met (i.e. the event occurs). You do not know when these events will take place at design time. All 3D games work this way.

RF is event driven. It is also object oriented. Every item that shows up in the game is an object. Every object has a set of properties which represent the object's unique characteristics. Some of these properties can be defined via the graphical interface.

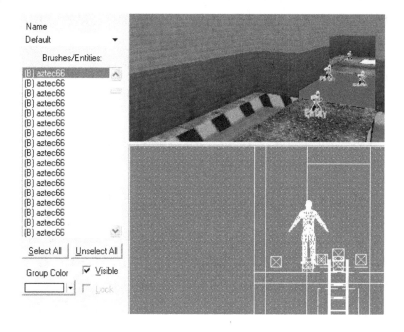

Separating graphic design from game design…

Game graphic design is a very time consuming process. Once you are into the graphic design process, the entire game creation process will slow down. A common problem is for the programming team to wait for finished artworks and animations from the media team prior to putting things together.

Assuming what you have got is a small team, I would suggest that you clearly break down the game creation process into two sub-processes, with one focusing on the logical "programming" side and another on media (graphics, sound effects…etc) development.

During level design, the programming guy does not really have to use "real stuff". Object actions and events can be designed and implemented through using simple artworks. Once the "programming" works are done and fully tested you may slowly import and "fit in" the real stuff.

Do I need to create animation for the game?

In RF, special effect (such as explosion) animation is possible through using sprites. To be precise, sprite animation is implemented in the media\bitmaps folder as a sequence of individual BMP bitmap files.

Note how the files are named:

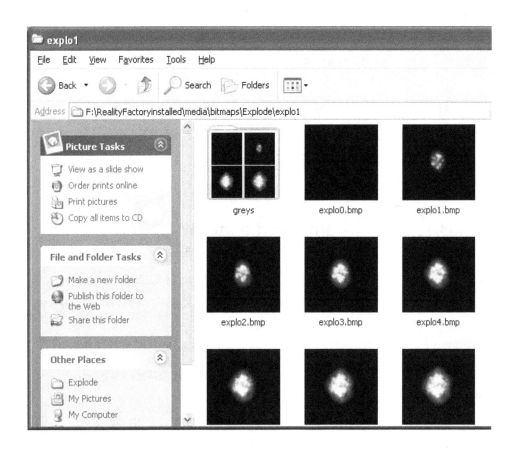

Splash video is different – you can use regular AVI file. You use splash video primarily for "story telling".

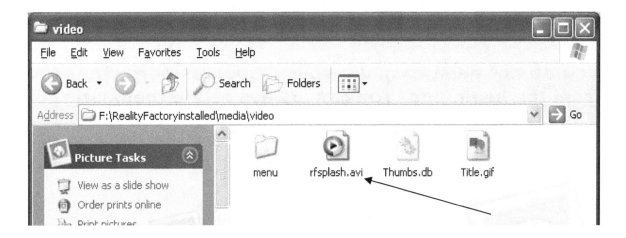

What software can I use to create animated sprites?

Most professional video or animation editing software can break an animation into individual BMP frame files. RF does not have built-in editor for this purpose.

Is animated sprite the same as animated texture?

No they are different. Sprite doesn't get applied on a 3D model. Animated texture, on the other hand, is for skin meshing only.

Should I start with resources first or game level design first?

You should consider items like sound, graphics, 3D models...etc as media resources. A complete game level cannot run without these resources or the level will present an empty world. I would say, at the time you plan your game level design you should also come up with some initial basic design of your resources.

You do not need to make your resources perfectly right from the beginning. You can always refine them later.

FYI, by default all media contents of RF are stored under this directory structure:

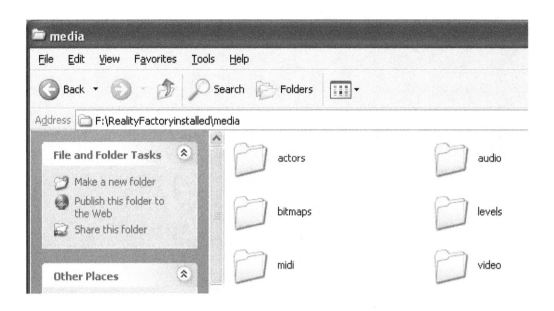

Why is 3DT file important in a RF project? How about the BSP file

and the map file?

3DT is the file format for game level design. The RF editor uses 3DT files to store game levels. The 3DT format is text based (that is why it is usually small). It describes a game level.

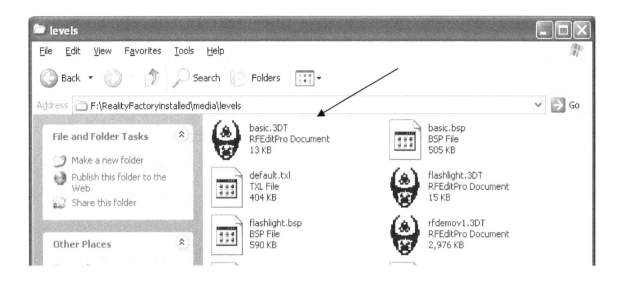

The actual game data is stored in the BSP file. Along the process of creating a BSP file a MAP would have to be generated, although this MAP file is of a temporary nature.

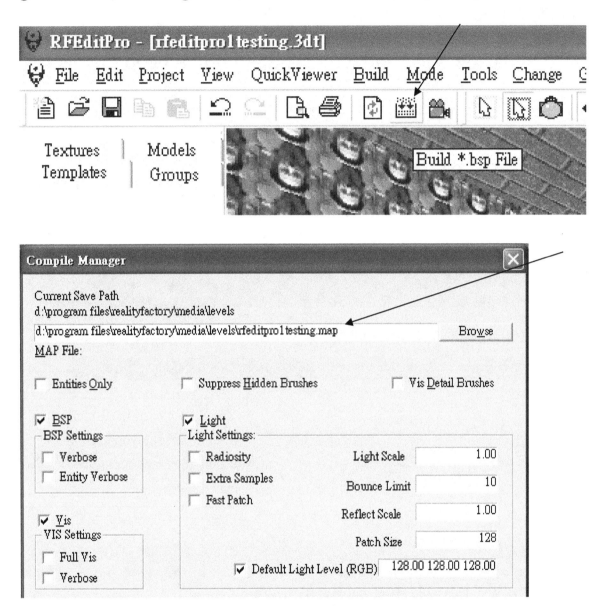

The .BSP file format is often used in games that implement Quake derived 3D engines. It uses binary space partitioning for generating levels that can be rendered quickly while keeping the number of polygons that need to be redrawn for screen refreshes to the minimum. To create BSP file there is usually a need to first compile a .MAP file.

Since RF is going to handle these, all that you need to worry about is the 3DT file. RF will use the 3DT file to generate the necessary BSP file and MAP file as needed.

Do keep in mind, for the BSP file to be successfully built, you need to get all the paths right, especially the so called "header file" (if you know the C language you should know what a header file is for):

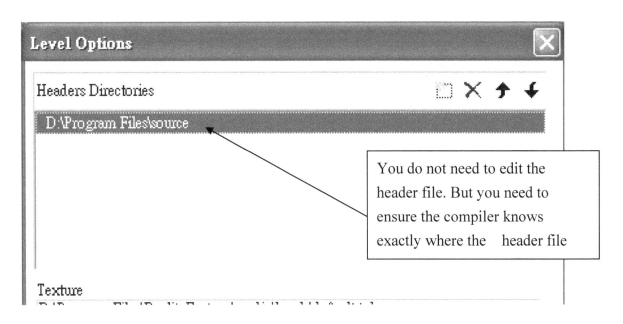

This is how a header file looks like:

```
/************************************************************************
****************/
/// @file GameEntityDataTypes.h
/// @brief Reality Factory Entity Data Types
///
/// This file contains all of the game entity data type declarations,
/// suitable for use by GEdit and the game itself.
/// @author Ralph Deane
//  Copyright (c) 2001 Ralph Deane; All Rights Reserved.
/************************************************************************
****************/

//      Disable unknown pragma warnings (GEdit #pragmas used here)

#pragma warning( disable : 4068 )

#ifndef __RGF_GAMEENTITYDATATYPES_H_
#define __RGF_GAMEENTITYDATATYPES_H_

#include "genesis.h"

//      Typedefs
```

There are other guidelines to follow for compiling a level, and we will deal with them later in this book. Assuming compilation is successful, you will see the following message at the lower half of the screen:

```
 ** BSP Compile Version: 15
** Build Date/Time: Jan 31 2005,06:32:56
 --- Load Brush File ---
Num Solid Brushes        :      6
Num Cut Brushes          :      0
Num Hollow Cut Brushes :      0
Num Detail Brushes       :      0
Num Total Brushes        :      6
 --- Remove Hidden Leafs ---
 --- Remove Hidden Leafs ---
```

```
--- Weld Model Verts ---
--- Fix Model TJunctions ---
--- CreateLeafClusters ---
--- Save Portal File ---
--- Create Area Leafs ---
--- Save GBSP File ---
Num Models            :      1,      80
Num Nodes             :      6,     264
Num Solid Leafs       :      6,     360
Num Total Leafs       :      7,     420
Num Clusters          :      1,       4
Num Areas             :      1,       8
Num Area Portals      :      0,       0
Num Leafs Sides       :     36,     288
Num Planes            :     24,     480
Num Faces             :     16,     576
Num Leaf Faces        :     16,      64
Num Vert Index        :     66,     264
Num Verts             :     19,     228
Num FaceInfo          :      4,     256
Num Textures          :      2,     104
Motion Data Size      :             40
Tex Data Size         :          52226
--- Vis GBSP File ---
Loading Portal File : D:\Program
Files\RealityFactory\media\levels\rfeditpro1testing.GPF
NumPortals            :      0
Starting to Vis all Leafs
Collect Leaf Vis Bits for leaf 0
Total visible areas          :      1
Average visible from each area:      1
```

Compile successfully completed

If, however, you receive the following message or something similar, you will have to check your level design to fix leak and/or other problems:

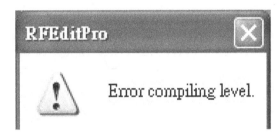

We will talk about leak later in this book.

I am confused – how do the terms brush, face, entity and hull

relate to each others?

First of all you want to think of the level editor as a model editor here. When editing a level, you will spend a great deal of time working with brushes and entities.

A brush is a basic piece of 3D geometry, which can be a wall, a staircase, a hollow box...etc.

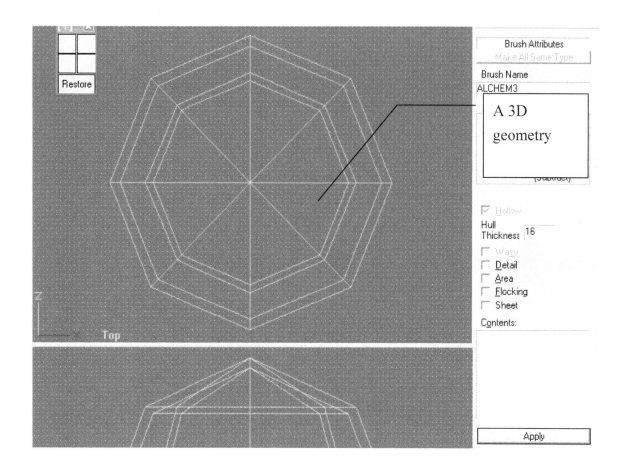

Solid brushes such as walls, floors, and staircases are for making up the building blocks of a level. Hollow brushes are similar in shapes. They are thin shells with configurable wall thickness (called the hull size). Cut brushes are tooling brushes for removal of material from the level or from a solid brush.

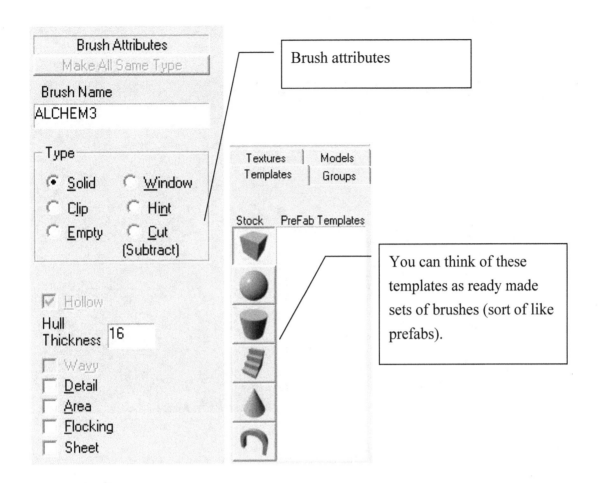

Brush attributes

You can think of these templates as ready made sets of brushes (sort of like prefabs).

By "assembling" these brushes you can build a level from scratch. You can also edit an existing level by adding new brushes to / removing existing brushes from it.

A brush is made up of multiple faces. Each face can be changed independently of the brush. Textures can be applied on the faces one by one, as well as on the brush as a whole.

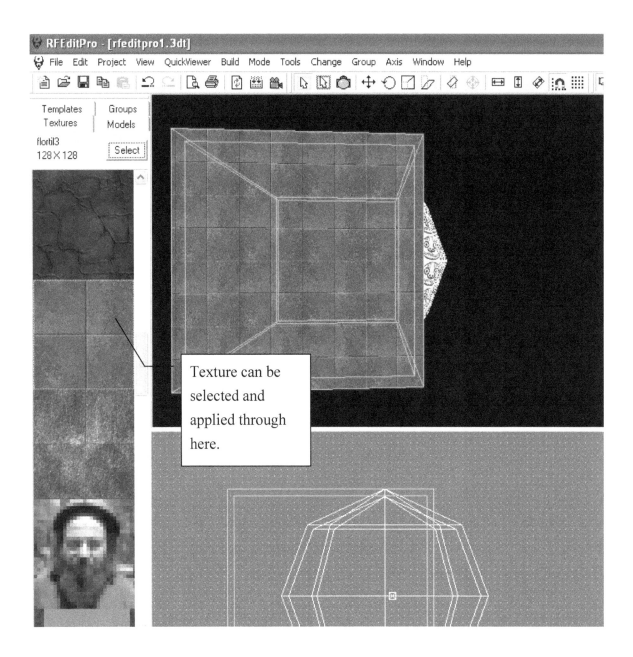

You may change the texture that is applied to the entire brush, or you may apply texture onto each face individually. Make sure you click on the select button and refresh the view to see the actual result.

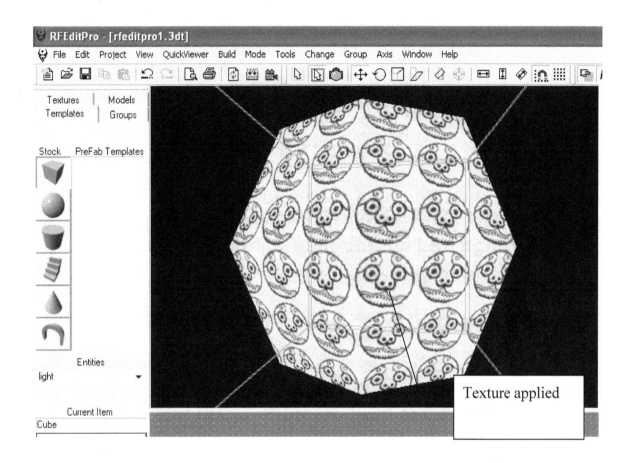

Texture applied

Entities are being referred to as point data. Examples include player start locations, level attributes ...etc. For lighting effects, the two explicit entity types available in the editor are light and spotlight. You use them to apply lighting effects to your level. Other entity types can be user-defined if you know how to code.

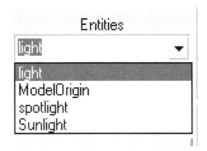

Generally speaking, you should build all of the 3D geometry for your level and texture their faces prior to going through and adding final lighting effects.

What are actors? What program can be used to manipulate them?

An actor is a 3D model which has motion. In the media directory there is an actors folder which keeps all the actor files. The file format is ACT.

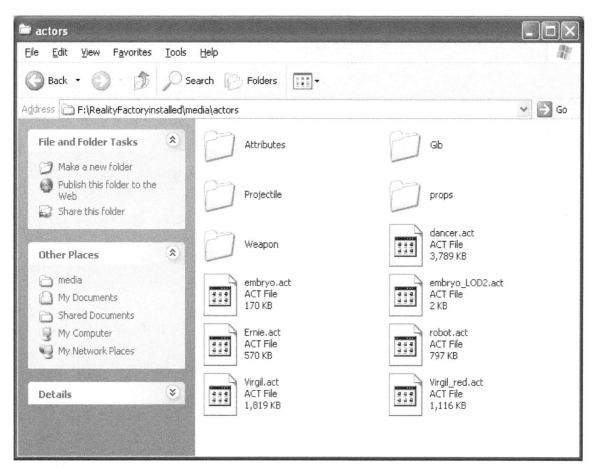

You may use the Actor Viewer program to read actor files.

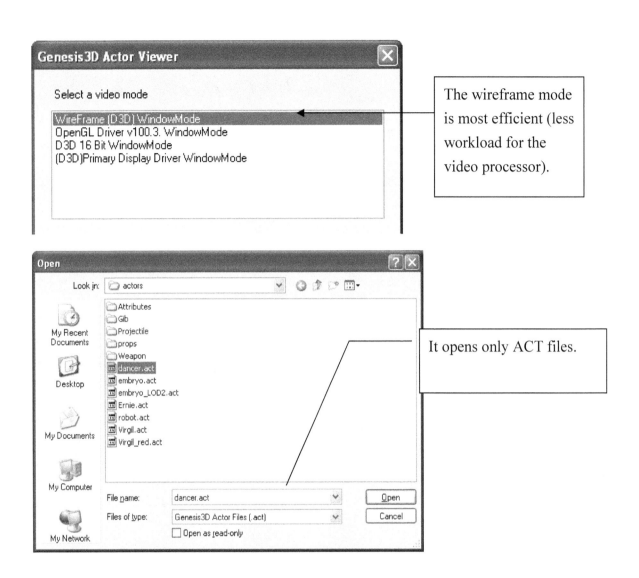

Genesis3D Actor Viewer

Select a video mode

WireFrame (D3D) WindowMode
OpenGL Driver v100.3. WindowMode
D3D 16 Bit WindowMode
(D3D)Primary Display Driver WindowMode

The wireframe mode is most efficient (less workload for the video processor).

Open

Look in: actors

My Recent Documents
Desktop
My Documents
My Computer
My Network

Attributes
Gib
Projectile
props
Weapon
dancer.act
embryo.act
embryo_LOD2.act
Ernie.act
robot.act
Virgil.act
Virgil_red.act

It opens only ACT files.

File name: dancer.act

Files of type: Genesis3D Actor Files (.act)

Open as read-only

Open

Cancel

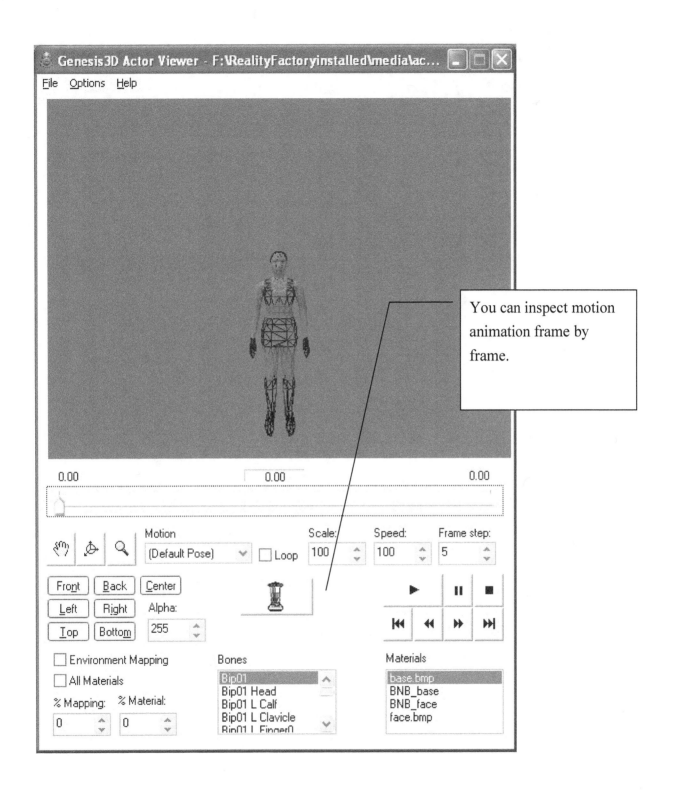

You can inspect motion animation frame by frame.

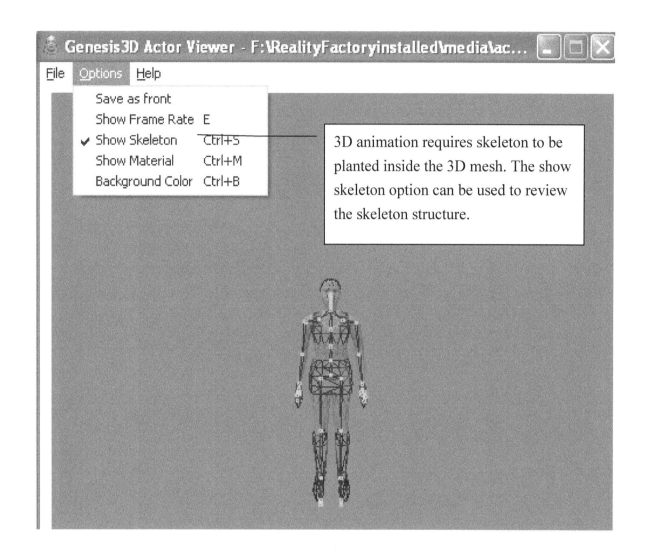

The program cannot edit and save ACT file (it is a viewer only). To produce ACT files, you may use Actor Studio, which is located in the tools folder. If you browse the tools directory you should see the astudio.exe file. Through it you can run the Actor Studio.

Actor Studio is most useful for converting 3DMAX file into RF's ACT file.

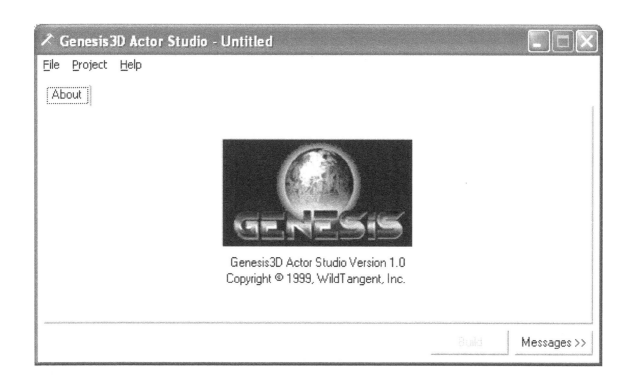

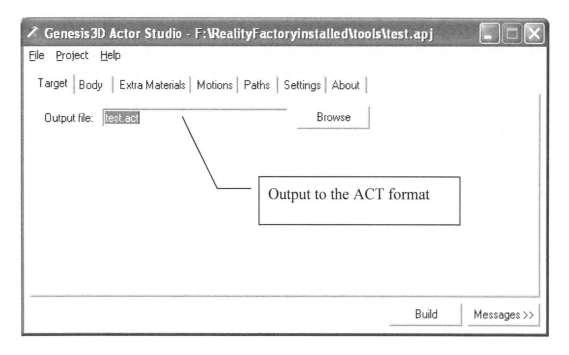

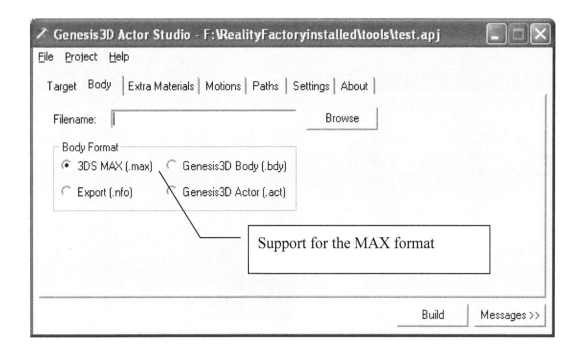

What kinds of bitmap file can I use?

In the media directory there is a bitmaps folder which keeps all the bitmap files. Their sizes vary. Bit depth is 24 bit on all of them, although for performance sake you may not want all your bitmaps to be 24 bit.

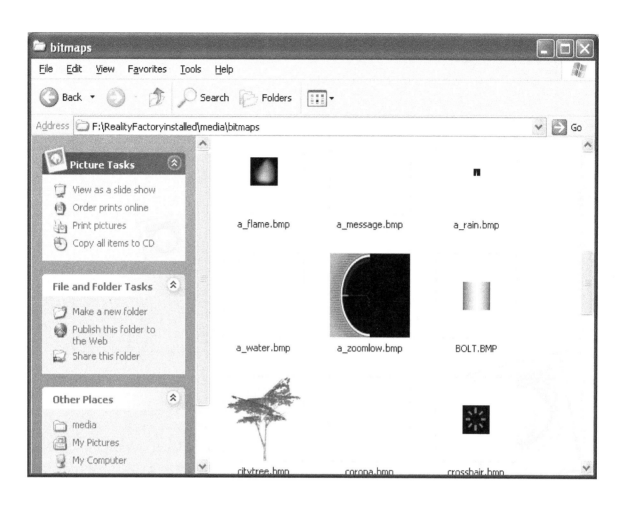

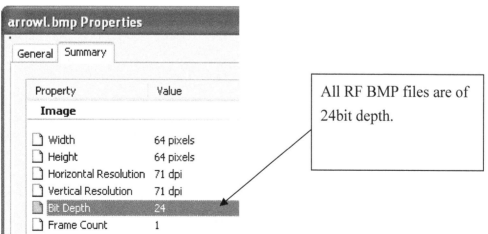

All RF BMP files are of 24bit depth.

Bitmaps are also used for creating the game text and the various menu items.

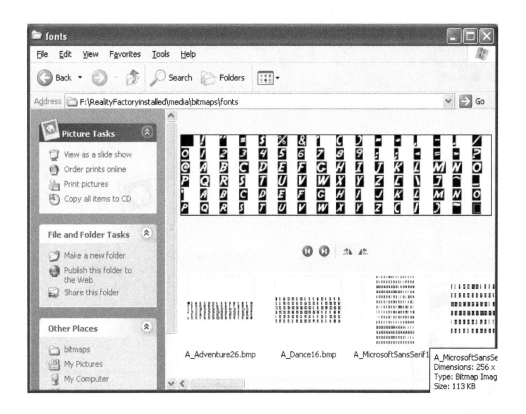

Copyright 2015. **The HobbyPRESS (Hong Kong)**. All rights reserved.

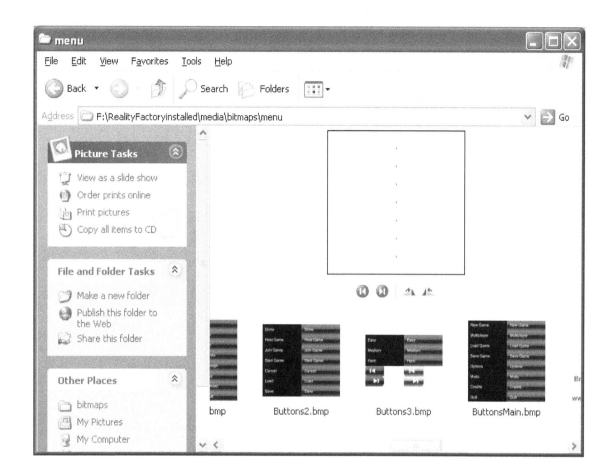

Can I insert the same object into the same virtual world multiple times?

Yes. Technically we call those as object instances. An object can have as many instances placed on the level as you like, subject to the limitation of the engine and the available system resources.

What is the preferred design-time display configuration in terms of

resolution?

Display size may be defined through setting the screen resolution. For 15″ monitors, 1024 x 768 is pretty common. For modern LCD displays, 1280 x 1024 is often being regarded as the minimum.

You are always free to resize the interface as you see fit. You want it to run in a very large window or even full screen for better viewing. Note that there is a video setup utility included with RF for configuring your desktop color depth and resolution:

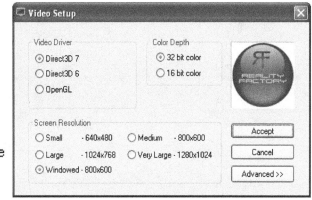

RF keeps track of the window config via its configuration file. You do not need to edit it unless you find a need for startup troubleshooting.

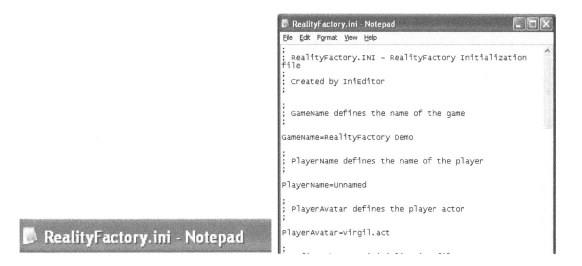

There is another ini file which is for use by the RF game demo. Modifying this file by hand is of no use since it will get over-written every time the demo is re-launched:

What is the default design-time display color depth?

RF supports 16/32-bit color depth setting. You should make your choice basing on available system resources. The more video RAM you have, the greater color depth you can opt for.

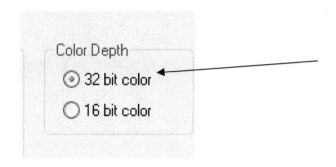

Why is full screen mode preferable? How do I configure the

runtime display settings?

When you use full screen mode the game will occupy the entire screen. The display system will focus its power on handling only the game and nothing else. If you run in Window mode (I mean a resizable/movable window, which is possible with RF), some other things outside of your game may run alongside, which can slow things down significantly (depending on what is being run and the actual runtime hardware configuration).

Do note that when you run in windowed mode, resolution will be restricted to 800 x 600:

```
┌─────────────────────────────────────────────┐  ┌─────────────┐
│  Screen Resolution                            │  │   Accept    │
│  ○ Small      - 640x480    ○ Medium  - 800x600│  └─────────────┘
│                                               │  ┌─────────────┐
│  ○ Large     - 1024x768   ○ Very Large - 1280x1024│ Cancel   │
│                                               │  └─────────────┘
│  ⊙ Windowed - 800x600  ◄──────────────────    │  ┌─────────────┐
│                                               │  │ Advanced >> │
└─────────────────────────────────────────────┘  └─────────────┘
```

How should I size my level map?

A RF game works in the unit of level. There is nothing to stop you from building a very big virtual world level. However, small is beautiful and it is always a good idea to not make a single place too over-crowded.

The size of a level is more of a game design concern. Technical constraint is a factor to consider but good game play is even more important.

Development Tools Configuration

What configuration should I use for my RF development station?

A development station for RF does not have to be real fast and powerful. RF itself is not a power hungry application. The thing is, you may need to do a lot of graphic works (2D for texture bitmaps and 3D for models). Graphic and modeling software can eat up processing resources crazily.

I think a reasonable configuration for elementary level game creation in the modern days would entail, at the least, a P4 (or Celeron) processor, 2GB RAMs, 100GB+ hard disk ...etc. To be practical in terms of performance, however, go with a dual core setup and more RAMs:

Intel(R) Celeron(R) CPU G530 @ 2.40GHz 2.40 GHz

8.00 GB

Concerning processor speed, you want to understand that the RF UI has to maintain 4 windows at the same time. If you move one object in one window, updates and recalculations will have to be made on all windows. This is in fact very demanding in terms of computational power. Therefore, a faster processor would be preferable.

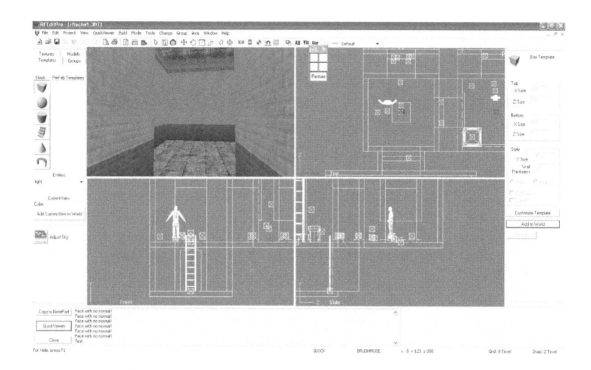

As previously mentioned, there is always a textured view that shows a 3-dimensional rendering of the level. Updating this view is a heavy job for both the processor and the graphic processor on your video card (the GPU). To save time when displaying the level in the editor this Textured view does not display any effects of lighting by default.

Storage-wise I always recommend that you have at least TWO hard disks installed on the same computer, with Norton GHOST (a disk cloning program) in place to create a complete image of your primary disk so if something goes wrong you can recover the development settings quickly by restoring from the image.

Working data backup is different – you need to regularly backup your working data into at least TWO different places, such as a high capacity SD card and a USB connected external hard disk. SCSI, IDE, SATA... all these don't really matter. RF will not run better just because it is on a SCSI disk.

What is the disk space requirement and directory structure of RF?

Without a library of fancy textures and models the default RF installation is rather small. If you are using NTFS compression the actual installed size on disk is around 50MB. Without NTFS compression you need about 100MB free space.

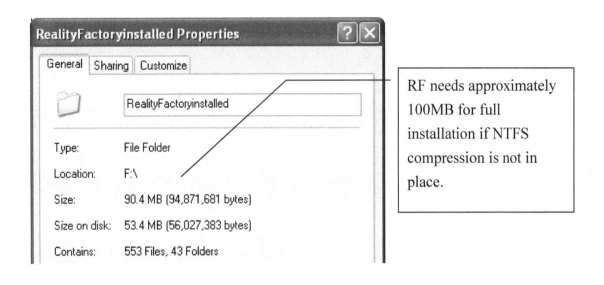

RF needs approximately 100MB for full installation if NTFS compression is not in place.

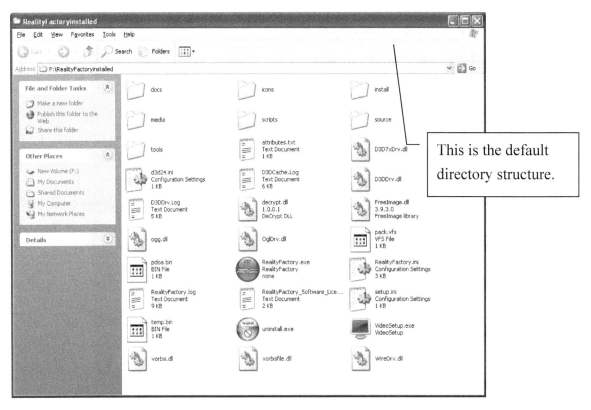

This is the default directory structure.

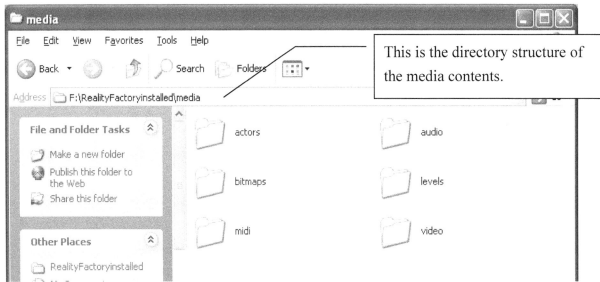

This is the directory structure of the media contents.

What is the recommended disk layout for my RF development

station?

Personally I would suggest that you maintain the following partitions:

- a partition for the Windows OS
- a partition for RF and all other development tools
- a partition for all the working data (game graphics, the game application files, sound effect files ...etc)

If you have a second hard disk, on this second disk you should have:

- a partition for Norton Ghost to build and keep clone images
- a partition for making backups of the working data
- a partition for Windows virtual memory (i.e. disk swapping)
- a partition for special purpose swapping (when you use heavy duty graphic processing application like Photoshop then you will need this for sure)

How much disk space should I keep for RF?

I would say you better keep 2GB or so just for everything RF related if you will be adding custom bitmaps and sounds.

For your data partition, it always doesn't hurt to keep as much free space as possible. Disk space is CHEAP these days anyway.

Design-end performance VS user-end performance

When you plan your development station configuration, keep in mind that design time performance boost is not the same as runtime performance improvement.

Design time performance boost improves productivity (your tools run faster), while runtime performance boost allows the game you create to run faster on the client end.

If your game is going to have a large number of super fancy rich objects all showing up at the same time, slower computers may have a tough time working things out.

Having too many complicated objects showing up together at the same time will affect runtime performance.

The key issue is this – when you have a very fast development station, all games can run fast in front of you. This can actually mislead you into believing that your game could run as smooth on the user computers.

It may not be wise to assume that all end users are rich enough to own the latest hardware. One suggestion – get yourself a separate test station solely for testing purpose. This test station should be moderately equipped – say, a Celeron processor with 1GB RAM and a simple onboard display unit.

Test your creation on this computer and see how things go.

What amount of memory should I install in my RF development

station? Do I need a dual core processor?

Along the process of game creation you often need to keep multiple applications (graphics, effects, game...etc) running at the same time, therefore the more RAM you have the better (and RAM is dirt cheap these days anyway).

RF is a 32bit based platform. It runs on 32bit based Windows. The maximum amount of memory that can be utilized by a 32bit Windows is roughly 3.3GB. Therefore, practically speaking a 3GB configuration would be all that you need. Most modern motherboards can let you install 3GBs or more of RAM (2GB + 1GB or 1GB + 1GB + 1GB).

We do not find any official statement from RF on multi-core optimization. Therefore, if you are running only RF and nothing else then there would be little performance gain by using dual core processor. HOWEVER, as said before along the process of game creation you will very likely need to keep multiple applications running at the same time. Therefore, a dual core processor would still be beneficial.

Do I need a high performance graphic card in my RF development

station?

Generally speaking, onboard integrated graphic display is slower than a dedicated display card. This holds true for ALL windows applications. For running RF, however, most modern-day integrated chipsets will do just fine, as long as you keep sufficient memory as video memory.

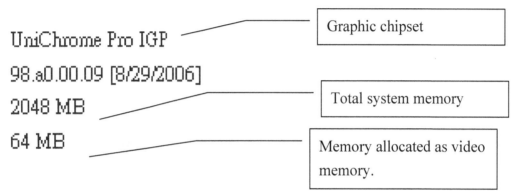

Higher end display cards using ATI/NVIDIA chips are quite affordable these days. And they are for sure DirectX compatible.

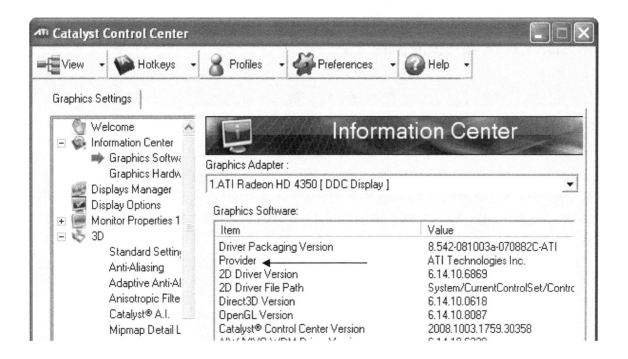

And keep in mind, design time performance improvement on your desktop may not translate into run time performance gain on the user end. What if your target users do not have the kind of highly powerful display card that you have?

I personally prefer dedicated display cards more simply because they have their very own onboard RAM so the main system memory can be conserved (no need to share memory with the display function).

Do I need a large chunk of Video RAM on my graphic card to

support RF? Do I need DirectX 9 or DirectX 10 installed? Do I need

the SDK? How about OpenGL?

Put it this way, if you have less than sufficient video memory your RF installation may still work, just that the outcome   will be poor (in terms of display quality).

Since RF can support very high resolution display at 32bit color depth, I would recommend a dedicated card with at least 256MB RAM on board.

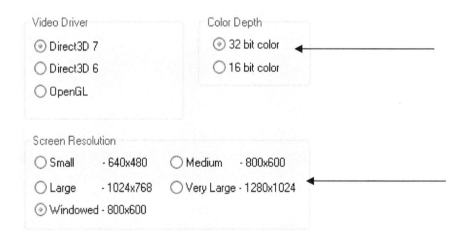

If you want your production environment to be of rich color (such as 32 bit color depth) and high resolution than of course you will need more Video RAM. Always remember, RF does NOT interact with the hardware directly. It manipulates your hardware through Windows. Therefore, hardware is more or less a Windows issue rather than a RF specific issue.

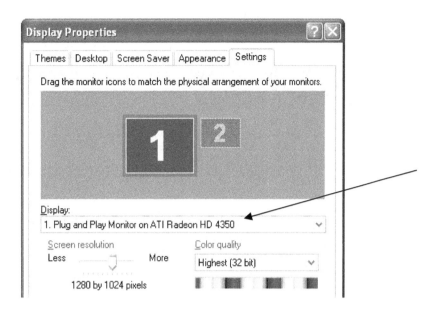

There is no need for you to install the full DirectX SDK (Developer Kit). RF does not need the full SDK. You also do not need OpenGL if DirectX is already in place.

Which Windows version should be used to power my RF

development station?

My personal recommendation is Windows 7. It is stable and reasonably reliable. Vista itself is way too power hungry. It eats up half of all system resources even when not running anything. Windows Server 2003 is never optimized for front end application like RF.

64Bit Windows 7 can let you use more RAMs. However, we have not tested it with RF. RF for sure runs fine in the 32bit version.

Do not run it on Windows 8. Windows 8 is not a good choice of OS for development purpose.

I want to run RF on a non-Windows workstation. Is it possible?

No. RF needs native DirectX support so you must have it run on Windows.

Windows XP Service Pack issue

Some people on the internet had claimed that their software did not really work smoothly on XP SP3. If your RF installation doesn't work well under SP3, revert to SP2 or SP1. XP SP1/SP2 are relatively stable for RF. OR, a better choice is to upgrade to Windows 7.

Display Driver issues

You should always opt for Windows Certified Drivers. If you are using a high end display solution such as a NVIDIA display card, there are many settings you can fine tune. It would not hurt to try them out. You may want to pay particular attention to the 3D settings.

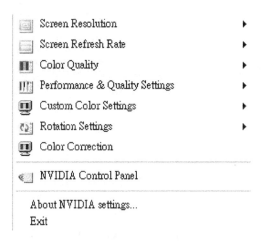

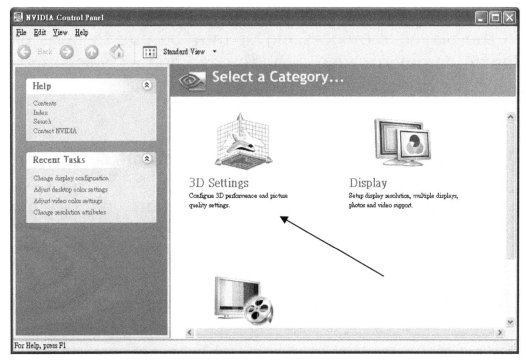

If you find certain objects occasionally missing from display, it could be that you are running out of video memory, or there is a problem with the display drivers.

Set aside at least 128MB of video memory if you are using an integrated chipset. 256MB preferred. This can be done from the BIOS. See if it helps. If not, install the latest display driver and also the DirectX driver and retry. Some older SIS chipsets can let you allocate 64MB at the max, which may not be sufficient at all.

The standalone game crashes when progressing...

If the standalone game crashes during initial loading, I would say this is more likely a display issue. However, if it crashes when the player is progressing, it may be due to bugs of the engine. A common cause is buffer overflow. Try locating and applying the latest patches from RF.

Can I install and run RF without any active network connection?

Yes. However, without an active connection you will not be able to download updates and patches from the web.

If my hard drive crashes, what special procedures are necessary

so I can reinstall RF onto a new drive?

As long as you have the source file handy, you may reinstall RF at any time. You can always download another copy from the web anyway.

Is a sound card REQUIRED on the development station?

A sound card is NOT a must. However, without a sound card you will not be able to try out the sound effects. A 3D game without any sound is weird.

Are the RF application files vulnerable to virus attack?

As of the time of this writing, to the best of my knowledge there is no specific virus attack targeting the various RF application files. Still, for your peace of mind it is best to have a proper anti-virus solution in place. Do keep in mind, there are viruses out there capable of infecting binary files.

You want to have a good virus scanner for proper virus protection. AVG is free is and is pretty good. PC Tools Threat Fire & Anti Virus is also a pretty good choice (and most importantly, it is free).

If you are running Windows XP, make sure you apply the available patches and fixes so most security loopholes can be properly addressed.

What is considered as an "editable copy" of my game? What about a compiled copy?

Your game file in 3DT format is editable. An editable copy can be run and edited from within the RF UI. A standalone game is always compiled. You cannot load the BSP file from within the RF UI.

A BSP file built by RF is NOT an editable copy UNLESS you reverse-engineer (decompile) the file using some hacking tools. Once decompiled, the resources inside the game can be extracted.

I am having errors when launching the editors. What could have gone wrong?

All the editors (including those alternative editors obtained through separate download) have an ini file which specifies the relevant file paths.

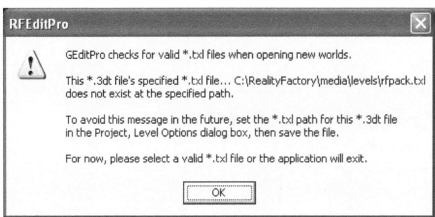

When your RF installation uses a drive and directory name other than the defaults, the ini file must be edited by hand (or through the Editor) to reflect your actual path settings.

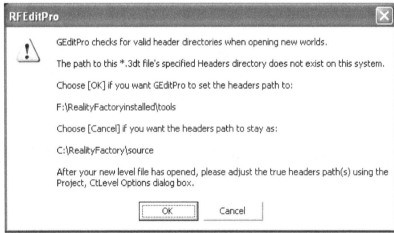

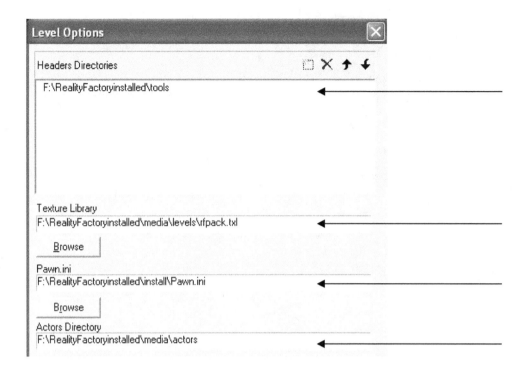

Game Design

How do I create the building blocks of a level?

Unlike other game tools, you do not add floor manually. By default there is already a box shape there. Think of this box as a container of a room. The empty space inside this box is where the game runs. You can resize this box, add more boxes to the inside/outside of it, or change its shape.

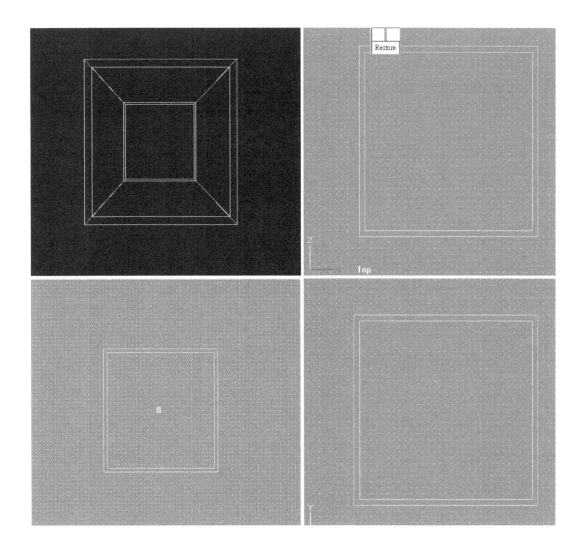

The box contains everything. There is no concept of "layer" (in the context of level map) in RF.

After selecting a texture on the left, you need to click Add to World on the right so the box is actually placed on the level.

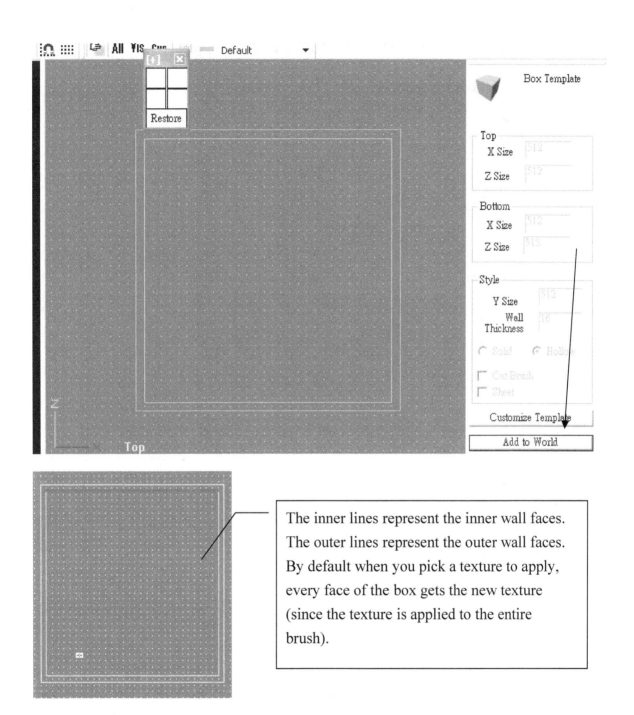

The inner lines represent the inner wall faces. The outer lines represent the outer wall faces. By default when you pick a texture to apply, every face of the box gets the new texture (since the texture is applied to the entire brush).

With the entire room selected you hit the page down button of the keyboard (or toggle between modes). You will notice a change in color of the lines surrounding the room.

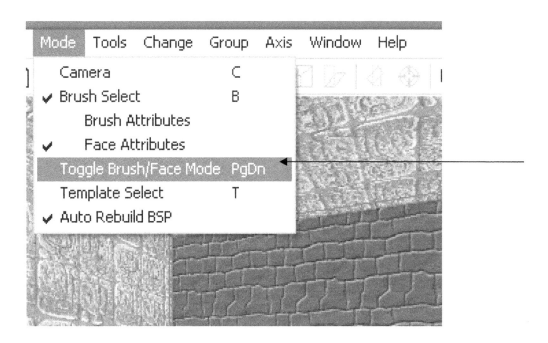

Now you can select an individual face. Apply new texture on a per face basis, then refresh the textured view to see the changes.

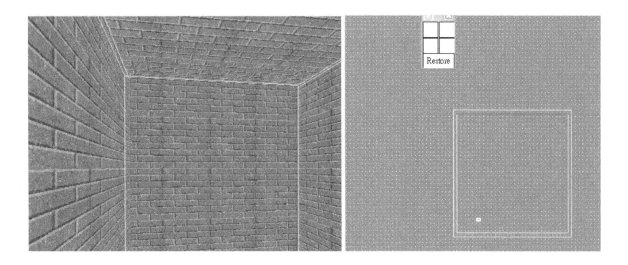

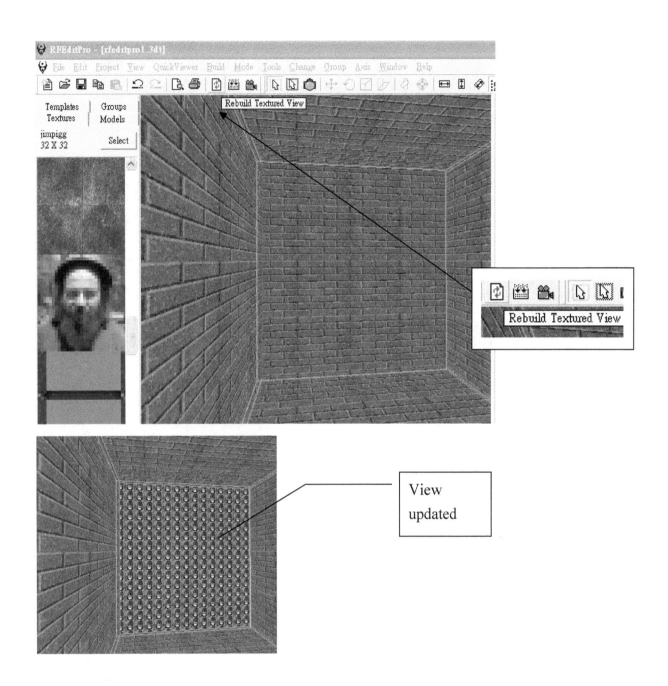

View
updated

You can rotate, move or scale the room using the buttons on the upper part of the display.

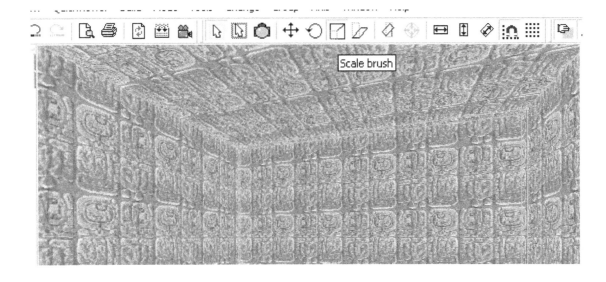

To ensure this level can compile, this room MUST BE solid. Otherwise, a compilation error will occur.

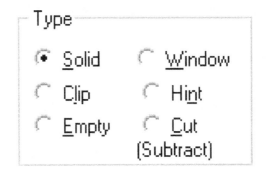

How do I add lights to the level?

Lights can be found from the list of entities. You can place as many as you like. The effect won't be shown in the textured view though (you will see a light bulb representing the light though).

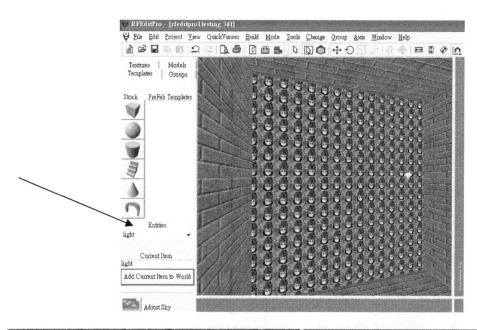

Note that these lights must be placed INSIDE the room or you will have problem compiling the level later.

How do I build complex shapes inside the room?

Refer to the following screen capture, a column is added to the room:

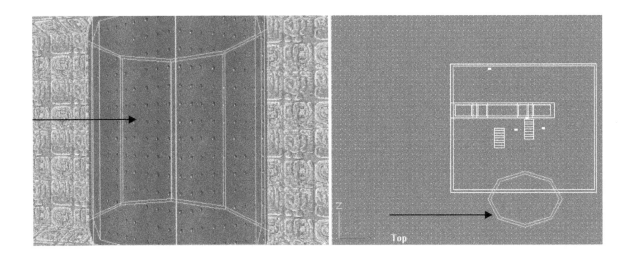

If you set its type to cut, it will cut off part of the wall and do nothing else. As a result there will be a leak and compilation will fail.

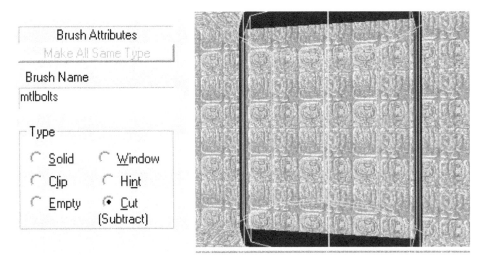

If you set the type to empty, the player will be able to walk into the column.

If you set the type to solid, the column will serve as expected (as a physical column).

How do I link up different rooms, and how do I avoid leak?

To build a larger level, you want to have multiple rooms in place. However, there must be no leak – that is, the entire level must be sealed. The best thing to do is to have one very big solid box as a wrapper which wraps everything.

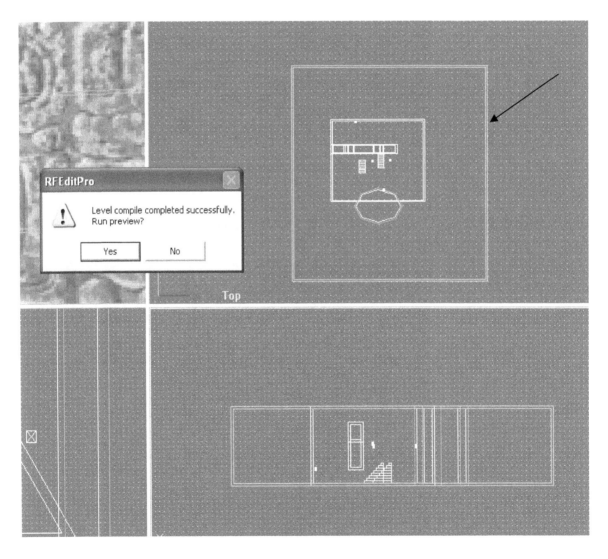

To allow the player to enter a box room, you need to make an opening on at least one side of the wall, by placing an object with a cut type that has proper wall thickness so it can cut away part of the box room's wall.

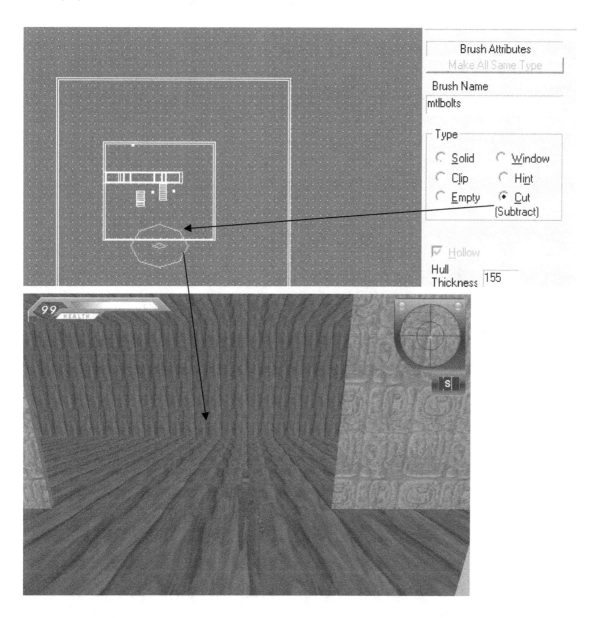

Another way of doing this involves customizing a template and placing it in between two rooms.

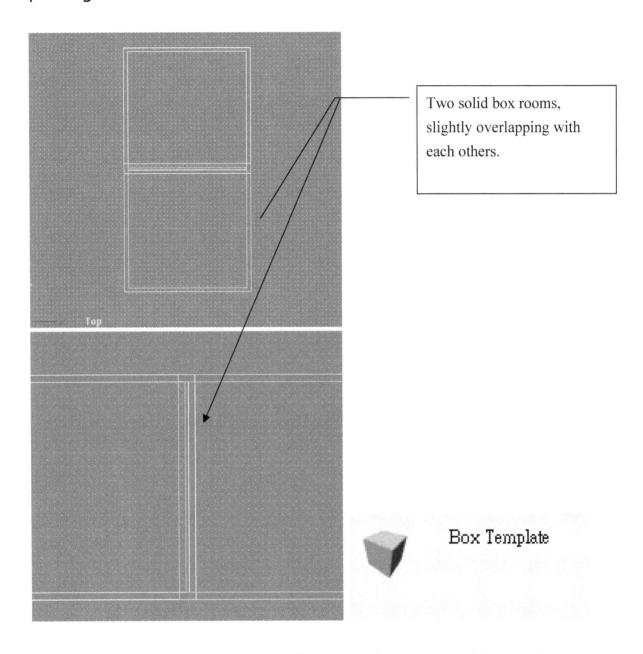

Two solid box rooms, slightly overlapping with each others.

Box Template

Now place a box in between them. Before you add it to the world, customize it first.

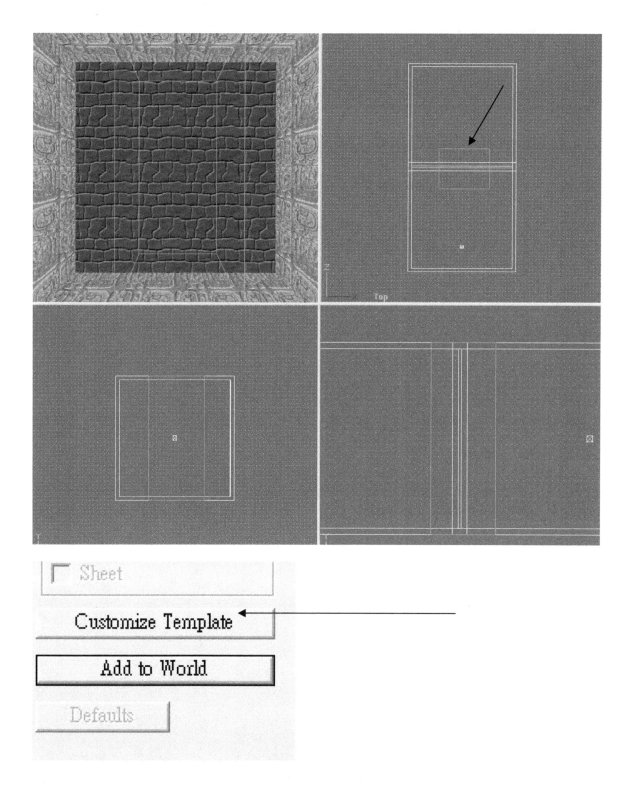

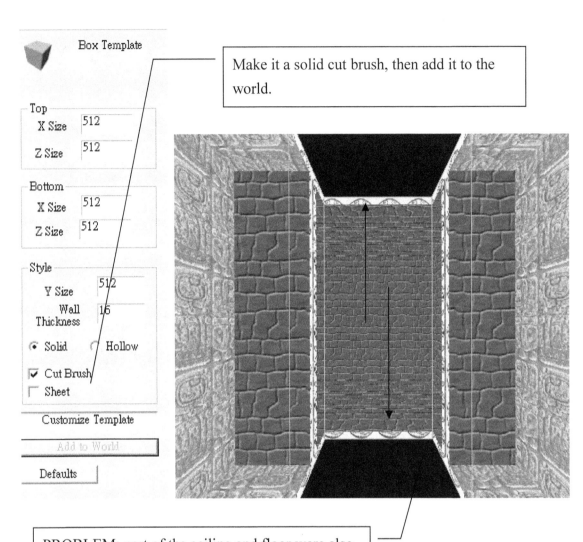

Box Template

Top
X Size 512
Z Size 512

Bottom
X Size 512
Z Size 512

Style
Y Size 512
Wall Thickness 16

● Solid ○ Hollow
☑ Cut Brush
☐ Sheet

Customize Template

Add to World

Defaults

Make it a solid cut brush, then add it to the world.

PROBLEM: part of the ceiling and floor were also cut off. That means we need to resize this cut box and make it shorter.

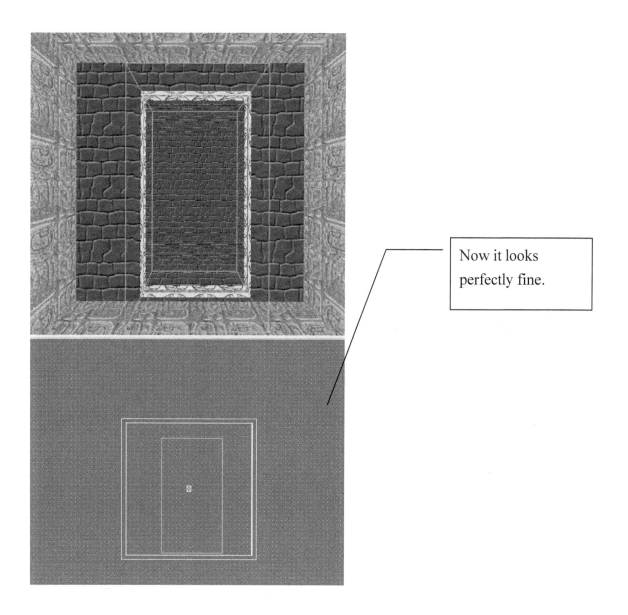

Now it looks perfectly fine.

To avoid leak, make sure there is no gap between rooms, and that all entities/brushes/cameras stay INDOOR (nothing stays outside). As said before, the world must be completely SEALED.

How do I setup a water pool, a mirror and a glass?

First of all you need a box template. When you choose the template you select liquid from the list of entities.

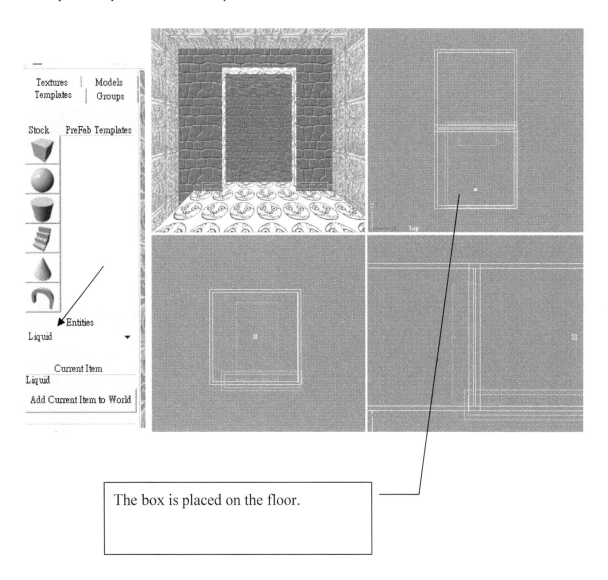

The box is placed on the floor.

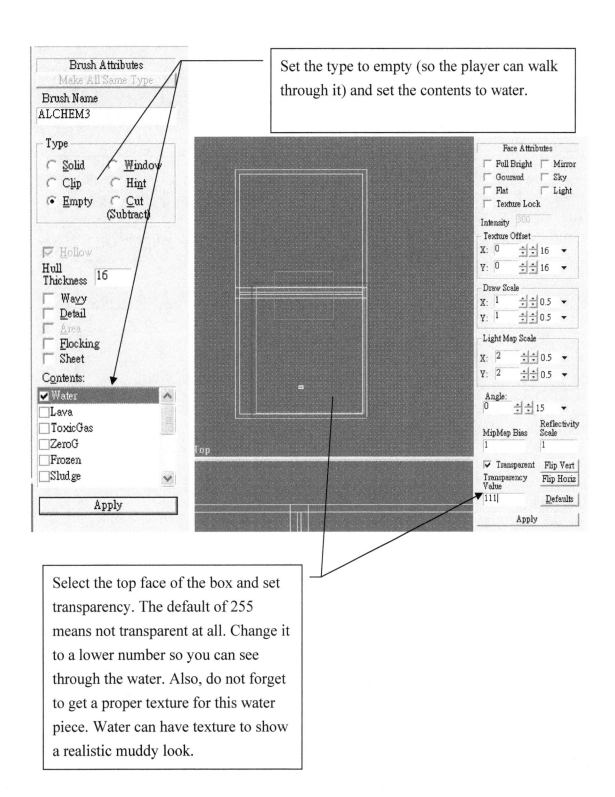

Set the type to empty (so the player can walk through it) and set the contents to water.

Select the top face of the box and set transparency. The default of 255 means not transparent at all. Change it to a lower number so you can see through the water. Also, do not forget to get a proper texture for this water piece. Water can have texture to show a realistic muddy look.

Creating a glass is simple. Just create a solid box and set the face to transparent, with a transparency value of, say, 140.

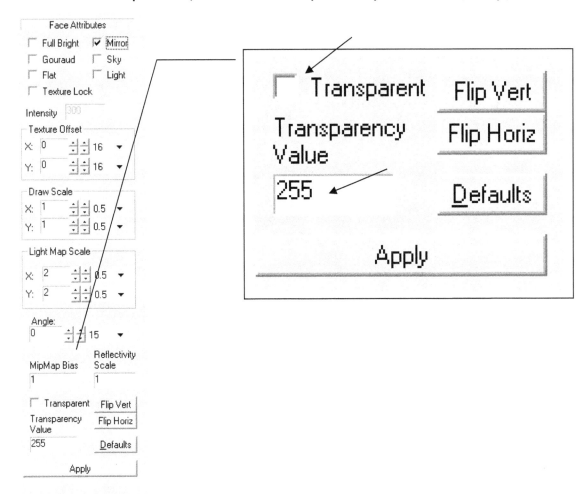

Creating a mirror is a little different. Since a mirror is going to reflect what is taking place in front of it, heavy computation is required. Having too many mirrors in your level will slow things down BIG TIME.

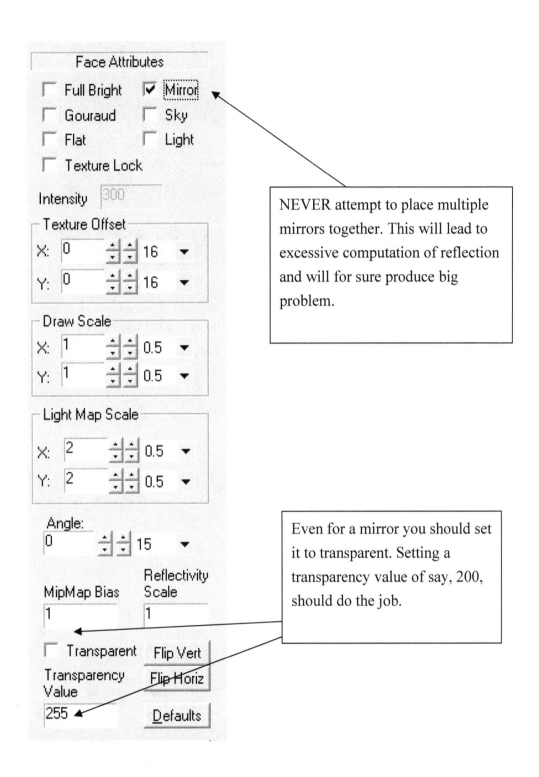

Face Attributes

☐ Full Bright ☑ Mirror
☐ Gouraud ☐ Sky
☐ Flat ☐ Light
☐ Texture Lock

Intensity 300

Texture Offset
X: 0   16 ▼
Y: 0   16 ▼

Draw Scale
X: 1   0.5 ▼
Y: 1   0.5 ▼

Light Map Scale
X: 2   0.5 ▼
Y: 2   0.5 ▼

Angle:
0   15 ▼

MipMap Bias | Reflectivity Scale
1 | 1

☐ Transparent   Flip Vert
Transparency Value   Flip Horiz
255   Defaults

NEVER attempt to place multiple mirrors together. This will lead to excessive computation of reflection and will for sure produce big problem.

Even for a mirror you should set it to transparent. Setting a transparency value of say, 200, should do the job.

How do I setup a player properly?

You need to define the starting point of your player. There is an entity called playerstart. To make sure it is made available in the list of entities, you MUST set the path correctly, otherwise many of the entities will be missing from the list.

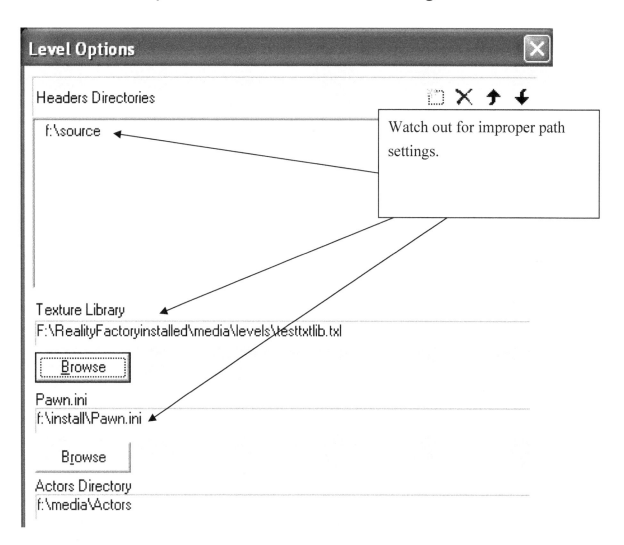

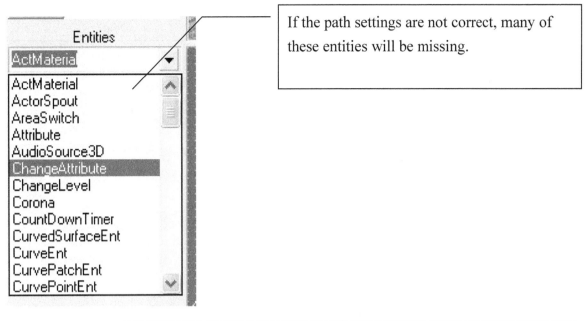

If the path settings are not correct, many of these entities will be missing.

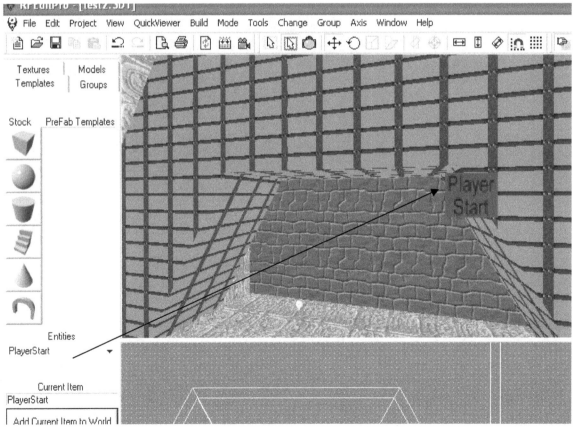

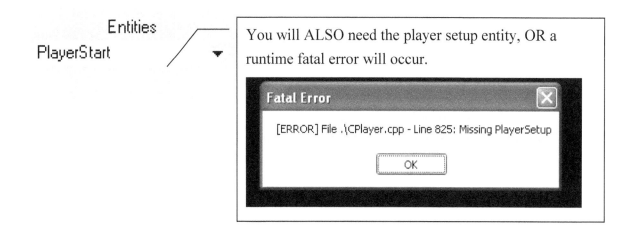

You will ALSO need the player setup entity, OR a runtime fatal error will occur.

Fatal Error

[ERROR] File .\CPlayer.cpp - Line 825: Missing PlayerSetup

OK

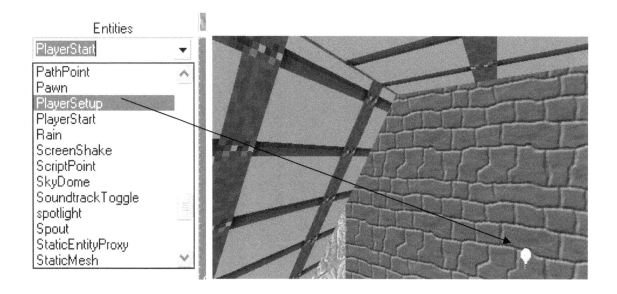

You do NOT have to locate playersetup right next to playerstart although it may be a good practice to do so (for clarity sake). It is not visible at runtime anyway.
Also, even though it is possible to put more than one playerstart on the level, by default only the first one will be active.

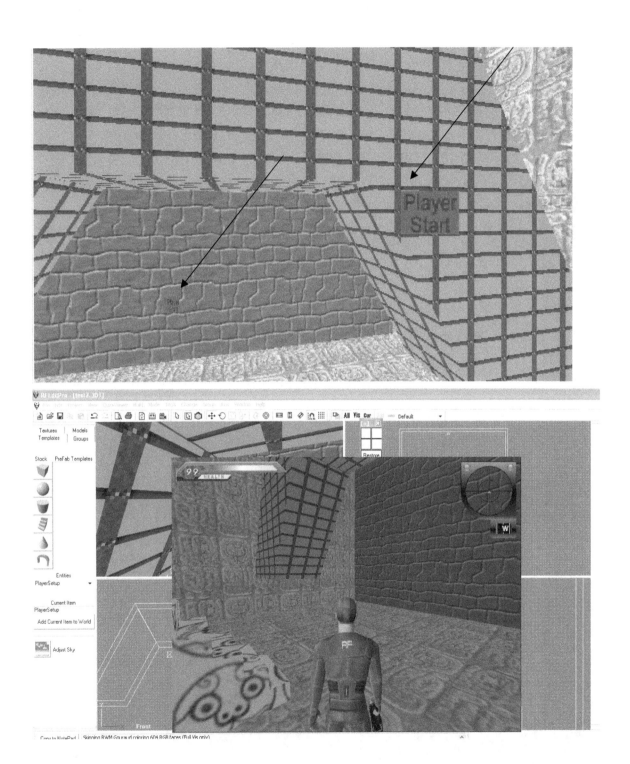

How do I setup a point for level change?

First you want to create a model. You need a model to be associated with a changelevel point (so when the player reaches the model the level change can take place). A model is basically a group of brushes. You group these models together so they can be referred to easily. You select the brushes to group, then click add model to create a model.

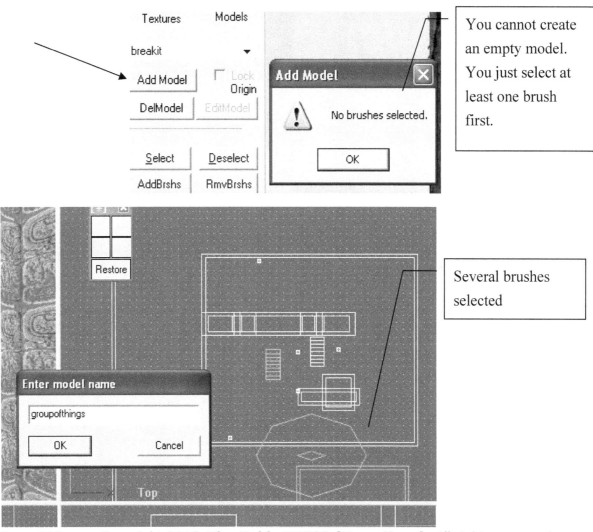

You cannot create an empty model. You just select at least one brush first.

Several brushes selected

Then you add a changelevel entity to the level. For the sake of clarity place it next to the model. On the right you can fine tune the settings of the level change. Pick the model that should be associated with.

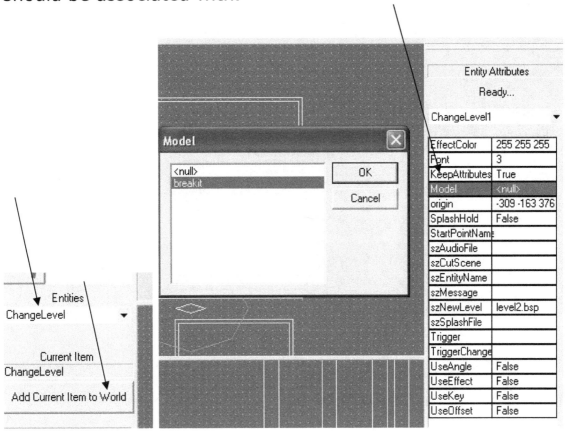

Also specify the complete file name (including the extension of BSP) of the target level. You may optionally specify cut scene, message, and sound effect.

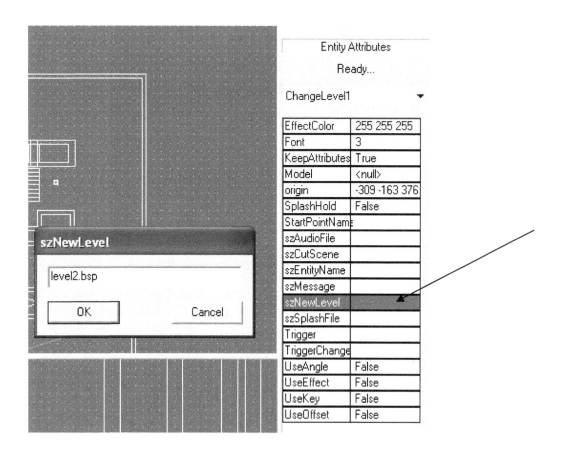

What sound format is supported?

RF supports WAV file, which is a very popular format.

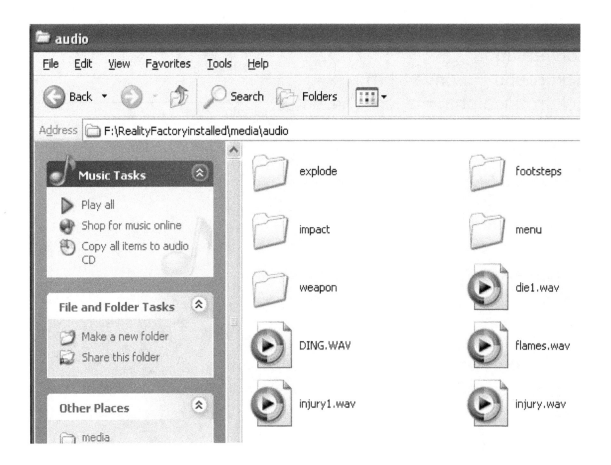

If you inspect the following ini files carefully, you can find references to some WAV files and you can make changes to those files if you prefer.

The pawn.ini file

;
; Pawn.ini
;
; defintion of all pawns goes here
;

;conversation defines

```
[Conversation]
background = conva4.bmp ◄──────────────────────
backgroundalpha = a_conva4.bmp◄─────────────────────
iconx = 0
icony = 0
speachx = 22
speachy = 20
speachwidth = 730
speachheight = 155
speachfont = 11
replyx = 22
replyy = 20
replywidth = 730
replyheight = 155
replyfont = 11
replymenufont = 11
replymenubar = menuconv.bmp
replymenubaralpha = a_menuconv.bmp
replybackground = conva4.bmp
replybackgroundalpha = a_conva4.bmp
speachwindowx = 16
speachwindowy = 10
replywindowx = 16
replywindowy = 440
giffile0 = menu\arrow.gif
;giffile1 =
;giffile2 =
;giffile3 =
;giffile4 =
;giffile5 =
```

```
;giffile6 =
;giffile7 =
;giffile8 =
gifx = 8
gify = 8




  .

  .

  .

  .



PlayerSetup.ini


;

; PlayerSetup.ini

;

; information used to setup the player

;


;

; 3rd person animation names

;

[Animations]

;

; default animations
; these can be overridden by the weapon animations

;

  .

  .

  ..

  ;
```

```
; player action sounds
;

[Sounds]
; maximum of 5 sounds per action
die = die1.wav
injury = injury1.wav
land = injury.wav
```

You do not use WAV files for everything as they are relatively big in size. Midi files (in mid format) can be used as background music since they are way smaller.

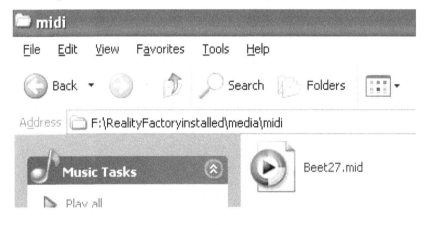

What is the pawn configuration file for?

This configuration file has the setup information for your enemies. Do note that to add totally new enemy types to your level you will need to write scripts. Script writing is beyond the scope of this Vol 1 text and we will leave that to Vol 2.

To make use of any new enemy types (those to be placed inside the pawn sub folder of the actors folder), you will need to edit the pawn.ini file and register them there. See below for an example of the kind of information necessary for registering an enemy in the file:

```
[Virgilnew]
actorname = Virgil_new.act
actorrotation = -90 180 0
actorscale = 1
fillcolor = 255 255 255
ambientcolor = 255 255 255
subjecttogravity = true
boundingboxanimation = Idle
shadowsize = 35
```

How to add enemies to the level?

You need to use the pawn entity.

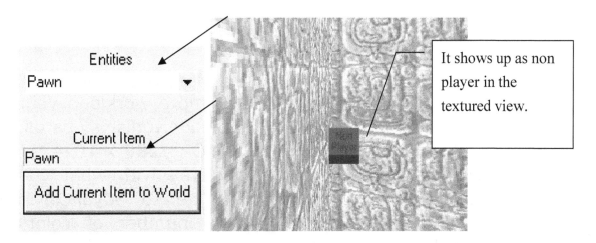

It shows up as non player in the textured view.

Copyright 2015. **The HobbyPRESS (Hong Kong)**. All rights reserved.

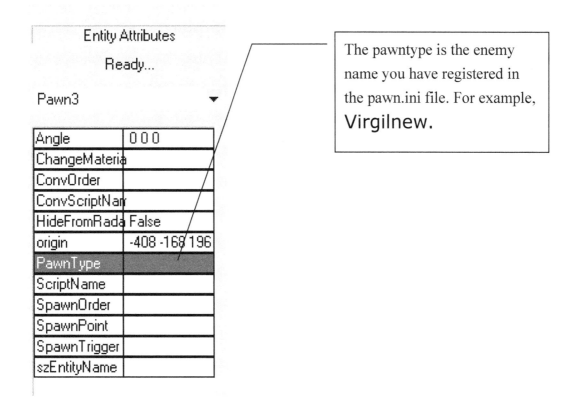

The pawntype is the enemy name you have registered in the pawn.ini file. For example, **Virgilnew.**

What is the optimal display resolution and color depth for RF to

operate at design time and at runtime?

In theory, the higher the resolution the more workload your display card would have to handle. Most modern display cards, however, will do just fine at 1024 x 768 OR 1280 x 1024. In terms of color depth, you may simply stay with what you already have in your Windows OS. Due to advance in hardware performance, displaying large number of colors should not really slow things down in your production environment, unless your display card chipset is very poor.

How should I define the runtime "minimum system requirement"?

If your target platform is Windows based PC, there isn't much to worry about in terms of "minimum requirement", since consumer desktop computers are so powerful and so cheap these days. Gamers don't live with slow machines. So don't let the minimum requirement concern restrict your creativity!

You may make the following assumptions on the client runtime environment:

- processor speed well over 1Ghz
- display card with 64MB+ of VRAM
- 1GB of RAM
- sound card
- plenty of hard drive space

What limits the display capability of RF?

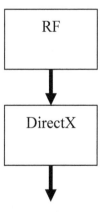

Copyright 2015. **The HobbyPRESS (Hong Kong)**. All rights reserved.

```
┌─────────────┐
│   Display   │
│  Hardware   │
└─────────────┘
```

RF works relying on DirectX. Therefore, things not achievable through DirectX are not going to be achievable with RF.

What compatibility issues can be foreseen with DirectX support

implemented?

DirectX is not perfect and problems can occur on different hardware platforms. There is simply nothing you can do about this.

When you distribute your game to your end users, you may want to include instructions on how to configure DirectX prior to running your game. You may as well want to provide your users with a link to download the latest DirectX software.

You may consider including the redistributable version of DirectX with your product. MS has a special download for this purpose:

DirectX Redist (June 2010)	6/7/2010
This download provides the DirectX end-user redistributable that developers can include with their product.	
DirectX Redist (February 2010)	2/5/2010
This download provides the DirectX end-user redistributable that developers can include with their product.	

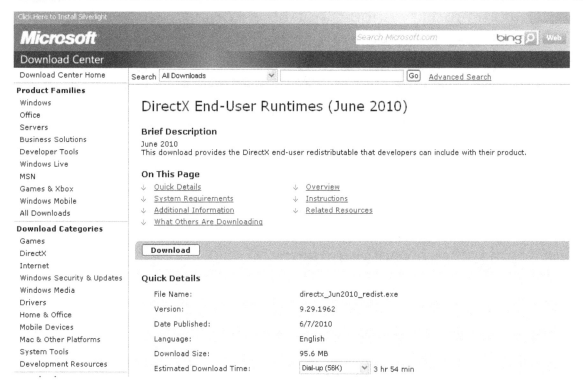

Display card driver performance issue

"I have a state-of-the-art 512M VRAM 3D graphic card on my PC but the RF game I created runs extremely slow for no reason."

If your game design is reasonable and the video card has so

much VRAM installed, I would say that a display driver update is all that you need to fix the issue.

Ask your hardware vendor to provide you with the latest display driver.

DirectX compatibility should not be a concern since all modern display cards are version 9 compatible at the least. You just need a good driver to work with it.

How to define runtime screen performance?

Frame rate is the key measure here. The more frames a game can sustain in any given time the smoother the screen display can go. RF game can have a frame rate of 58~ 60 under the following hardware configuration:

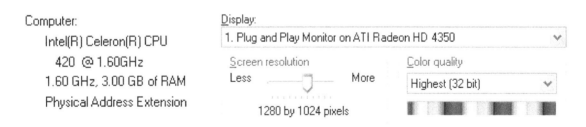

However, there are factors that can work against this:
● Corrupted DirectX driver on the client side
● There are too many complicated objects (high polygon count models) moving around on screen at the same time...

How do I measure actual runtime screen performance? What is the

runtime performance of RF game?

You need to use a special utility to measure the frame rate. NOT EVERY FRAME RATE CAPTURE UTILITY CAN SUPPORT RF GAMES. To measure frame rate of a RF game, we use FRAPS.

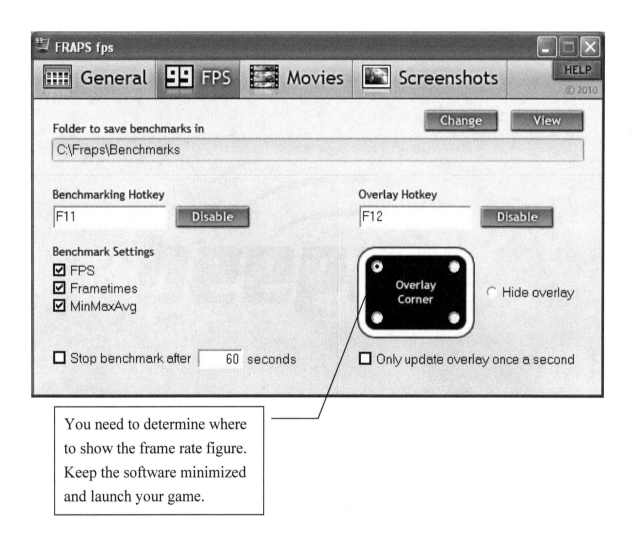

You need to determine where to show the frame rate figure. Keep the software minimized and launch your game.

When running the RF demo game in the highest resolution mode, a frame rate close to 50 can be sustained. Similar level of performance can be achieved when the game is run under the windowed mode.

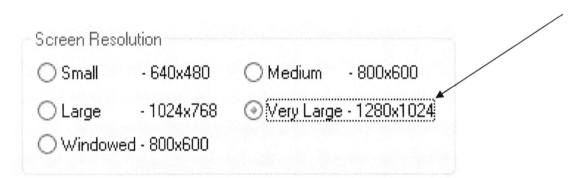

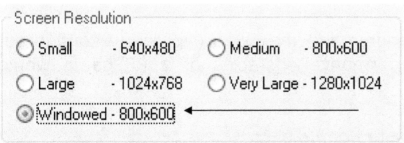

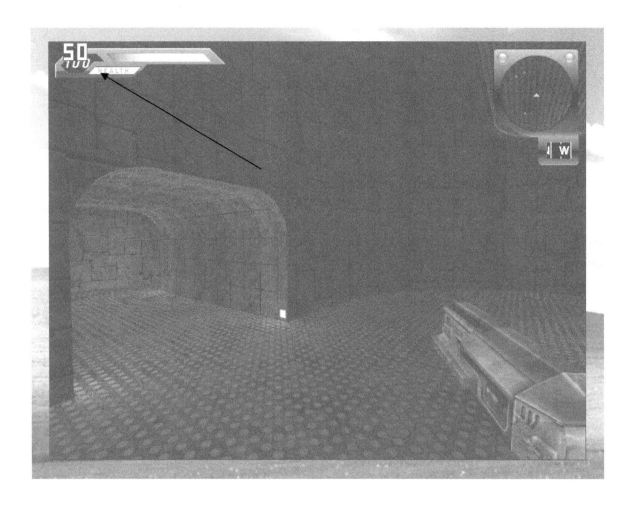

What are the major runtime performance obstacles?

Assuming the computer and the OS are properly configured, major runtime performance obstacles of a RF game would include:

- stupidly complicated game play
- unrealistic screen details, which tax the display function heavily
- overcrowded levels

- overcomplicated 3D models

You will see a significant drop in frame rate as a result.

Most 3D action games shouldn't require intensive computation unless there is some serious flaw in the program logic (bugs ...). Unrealistic screen details and the extensive use of rich objects may slow things down and this is more or less a design issue.

What is full-scene anti-aliasing and how would it affect runtime

performance?

Full-scene anti-aliasing (FSAA) can avoid jaggies on full screen images. With this feature, the displayed images may look softer and more realistic.

Some display cards allow you to turn this feature on and off by hand.

The video setup tool has an advanced section which allows you to turn on FSAA.

Screen Resolution

◯ Small   - 640x480   ◯ Medium   - 800x600

◯ Large   - 1024x768   ◉ Very Large - 1280x1024

◯ Windowed - 800x600

[Accept]

[Cancel]

[Advanced >]◄─────────────────

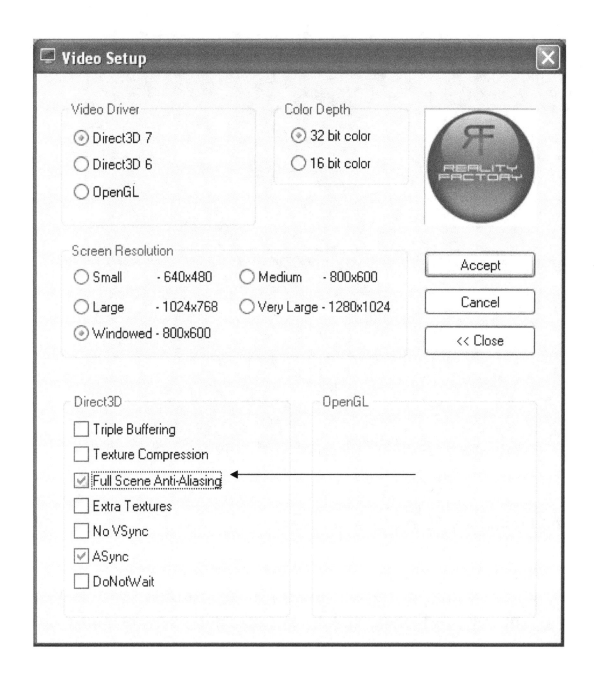

We have tested the RF demo with FSAA turned on (by default it is off). No impact on performance was observed.

How do I make my 3D models simpler?

For a true 3D engine, polygon count does matter in terms of performance. More polygons mean finer details and better looking models but way lower speed as there is more to calculate.

To effectively cut down the number of polygons in complex models you need specialized software. You just can't do it yourself. TGC (http://www.thegamecreators.com/) has a software called Action 3D which can do this job for you. The good thing about this software is that it can import and export models in a wide range of format.

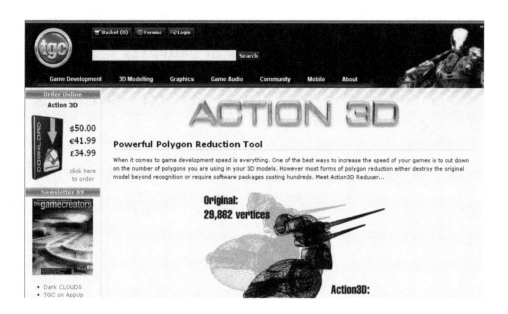

Why would I encounter an unexpected unknown error while the

game is loading?

Based on experience, some hardware issues might have produced the problem – it could be defective hardware, insufficient hardware (for example, running out of memory), problematic hardware driver…etc etc. When this error is encountered, load the game on a different computer (a computer with different hardware configuration) and see if the same would happen.

What tool can I use to open texture files of another format and

convert them to BMPs for further manipulation?

You need a conversion tool. One such tool is the LS Image Converter from Linos Software:

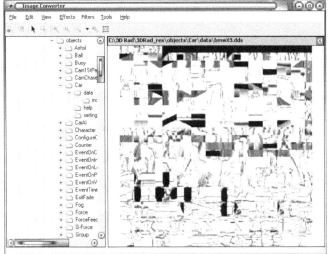

The Image Converter currently supports these image types:

IMPORT - PDF, PSD, PS, EPS, WBMP, WMF, EMF, PIC, JP2, JLS, FPX, RAW, DCM, CUT, IFF, DDS, PBM, PGM, PPM, RAF, RAS, XMB, XPB

EXPORT - BMP, JPEG, GIF, TIF, PNG, PCX, ICO, TGA, PSD, PS, EMF, JP2, FPX, RAW, PBM, PGM, PPM, XPB.

Smoothdraw is a paint program that can read file in a wide range of formats for editing.

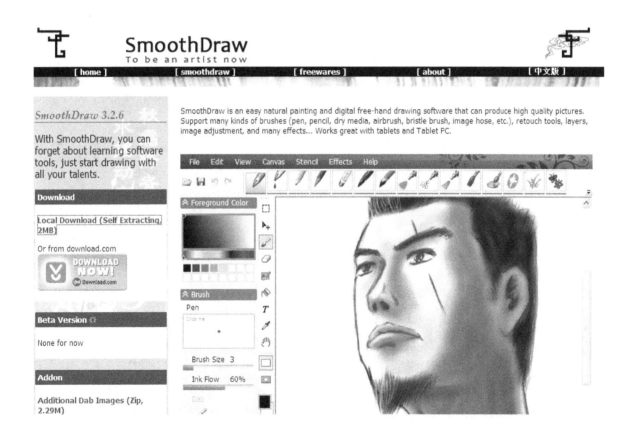

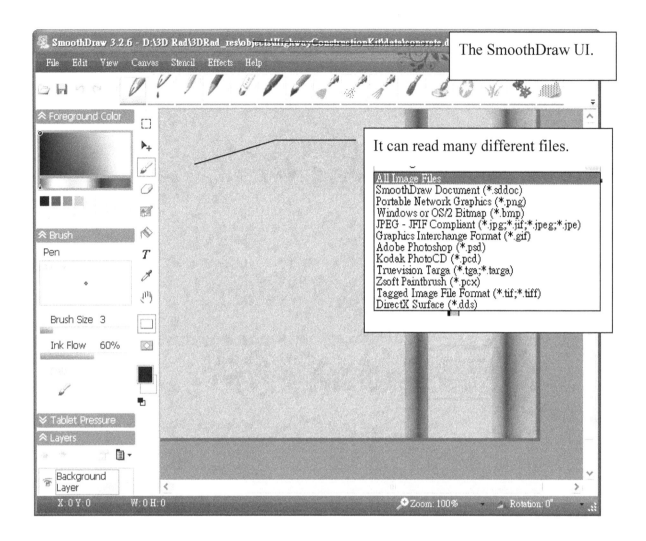

The SmoothDraw UI.

It can read many different files.

If you are making texture for wall tiles you should make them in multiples of 64, 128, or 256 pixels in size. Also, there is nothing to stop you from using higher color depth but at runtime performance issues may arise. For the sake of performance optimization you may want your BMP files to be saved in 256 Indexed Color Mode.

What tool can I use to create 3D models?

To create 3D models, you can use the AC3D software from TGC. In fact there is a trial version you can download:

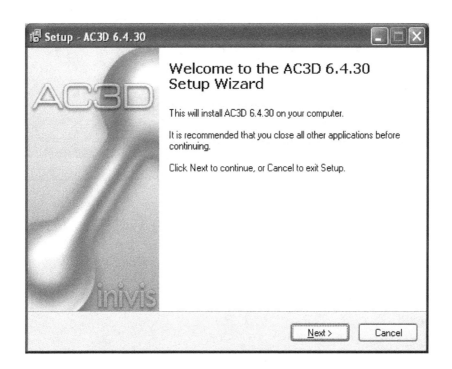

Copyright 2015. **The HobbyPRESS (Hong Kong)**. All rights reserved.

The AC3D main interface:

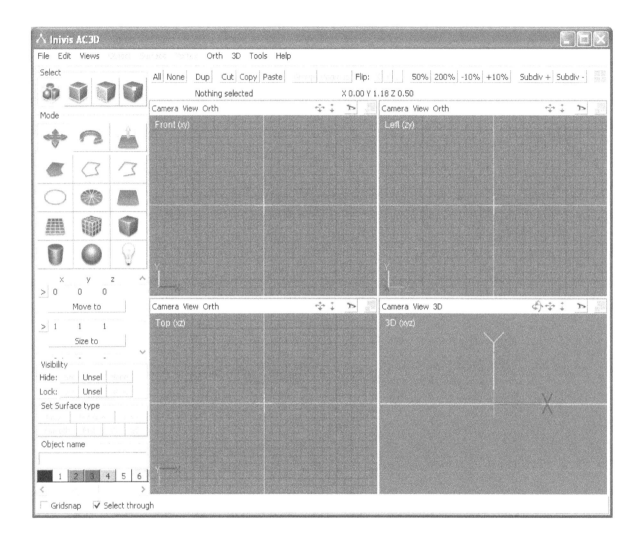

You can create or import models from a wide range of format.

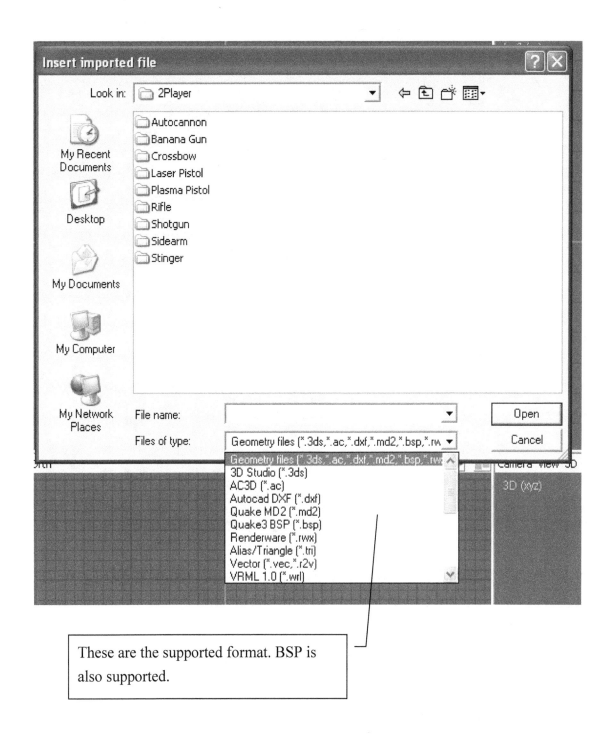

Insert imported file

Look in: 2Player

- Autocannon
- Banana Gun
- Crossbow
- Laser Pistol
- Plasma Pistol
- Rifle
- Shotgun
- Sidearm
- Stinger

My Recent Documents
Desktop
My Documents
My Computer
My Network Places

File name:

Files of type: Geometry files (*.3ds,*.ac,*.dxf,*.md2,*.bsp,*.rw

Open
Cancel

Geometry files (*.3ds,*.ac,*.dxf,*.md2,*.bsp,*.rw
3D Studio (*.3ds)
AC3D (*.ac)
Autocad DXF (*.dxf)
Quake MD2 (*.md2)
Quake3 BSP (*.bsp)
Renderware (*.rwx)
Alias/Triangle (*.tri)
Vector (*.vec,*.r2v)
VRML 1.0 (*.wrl)

These are the supported format. BSP is also supported.

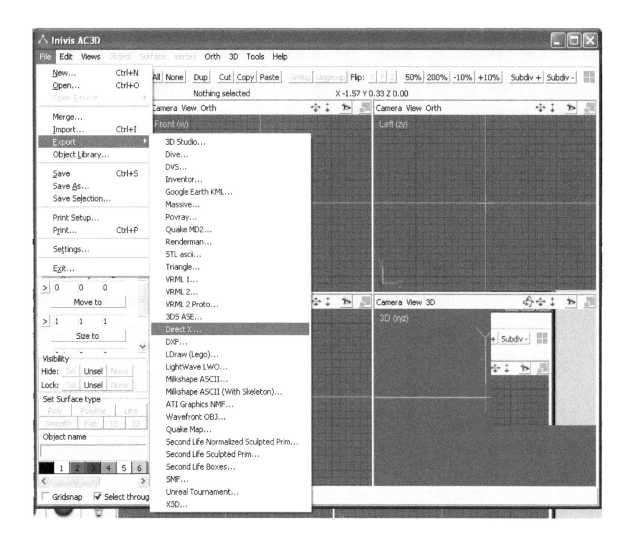

Other tools that can create fancy 3D models include Blender (http://www.blender.org/) and Milkshape (http://www.milkshape3d.com/).

Blender is an open source software for 3D content creation. It is totally free:

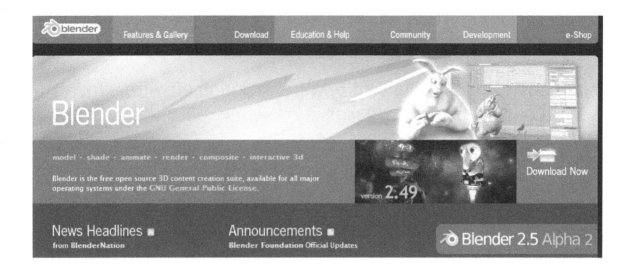

MilkShape 3D is shareware. It is a low-polygon modeler and also a skeletal animator.

MilkShape 3D Screenshots

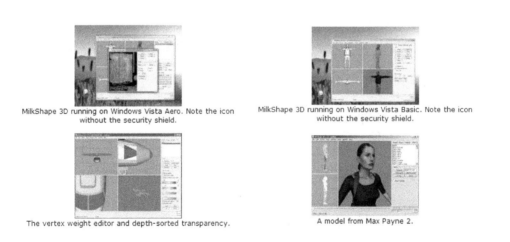

MilkShape 3D running on Windows Vista Aero. Note the icon without the security shield.

MilkShape 3D running on Windows Vista Basic. Note the icon without the security shield.

The vertex weight editor and depth-sorted transparency.

A model from Max Payne 2.

If you have $, you may also consider to purchase the 3D Studio Max package. It supports the MAX format and also the 3DS format. Through it you can take a 3DS model and export to the newer MAX format.

How do I create my own texture files?

You need to use specialized texture making software. One such tool is the Texture Maker (http://www.texturemaker.com/):

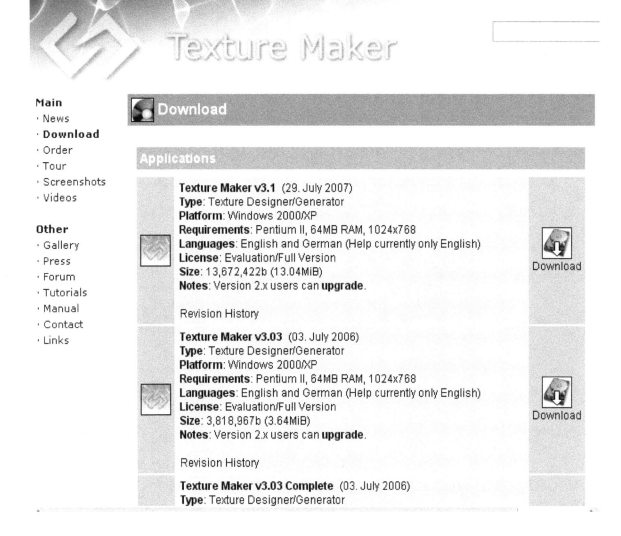

You can think of it as a Photoshop kind of software specializing in texture creation.

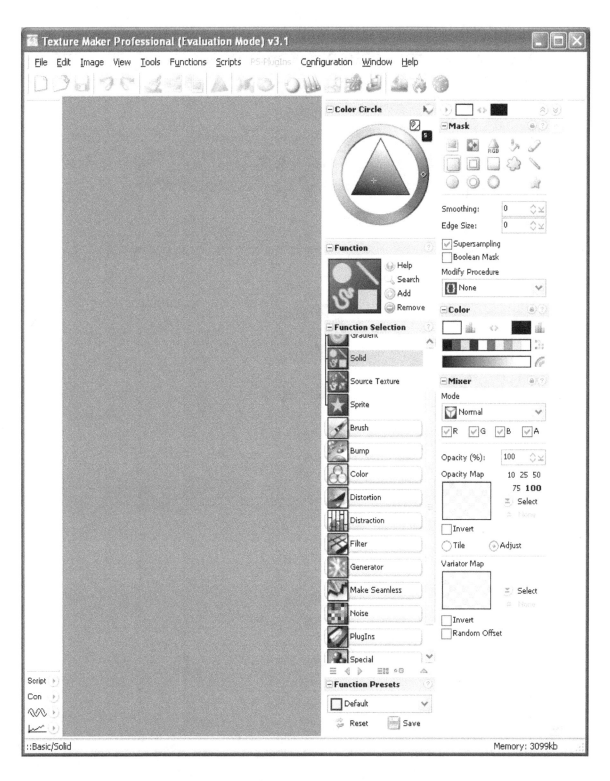

Once you define the texture size you can use the Generator functions for texture creation. Generator functions can render basic patterns and materials such as wood, stone, rock, water caustics, brick etc.

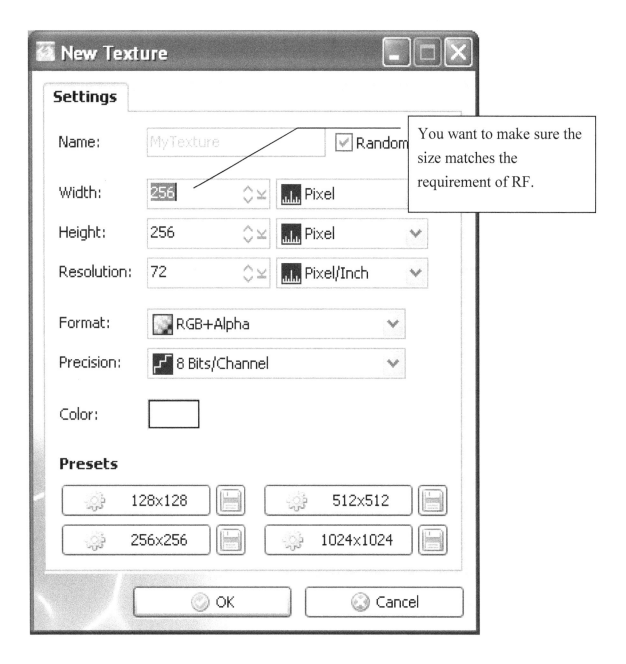

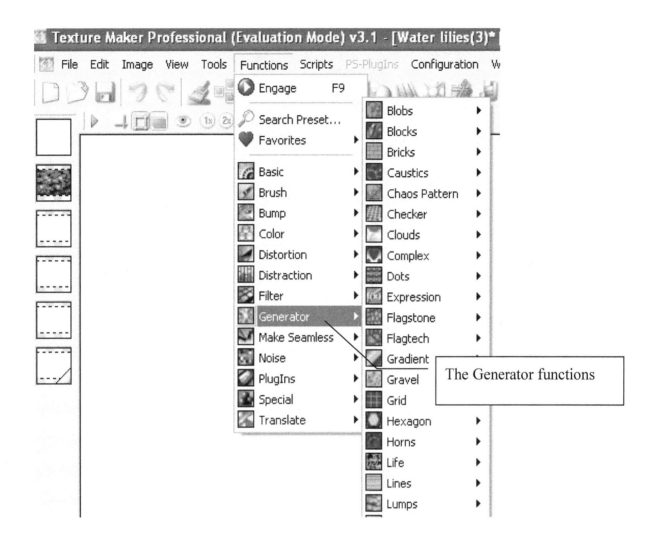

The Generator functions

How do I incorporate my own textures into the game level?

Inside the interface, you can scroll through the texture browser on the left and pick a texture. HOWEVER, the sources of these textures are not stored in their native format. The textures are embedded into the level files so you cannot add/edit texture by directly placing BMP files in the directory structure.

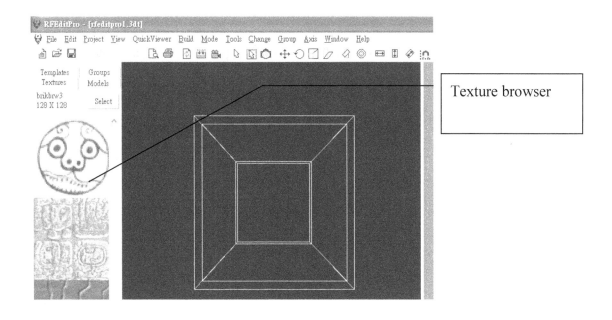

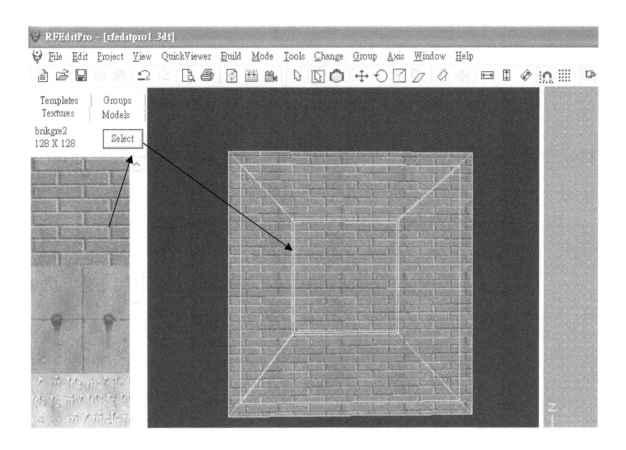

After applying a new texture you need to refresh the view to see the changes.

To add your own textures, you need to use the RF Texture Packer utility which is in the tools directory.

You drag and drop BMP texture files into the packer software, then save everything together into one TXL file.

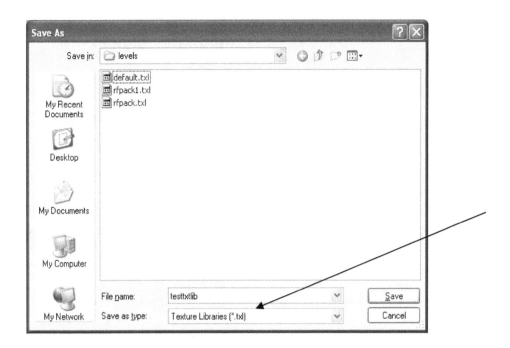

Then you need to update the level options to use the new texture file in the library.

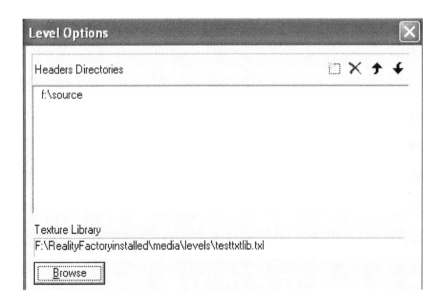

How can I make installation of my standalone game easier?

RF does not come with any installer utility so you must get one from a third party vendor. Clickteam has a software called Install Creator 2 which is good for this purpose.

http://www.clickteam.com/install-creator-2

You may download a free version to try out.

For the latest content update, please visit:

http://gameengines.net/

Please email your questions and comments to

editor@HobbyPRESS.net.

Index

www.ingramcontent.com/pod-product-compliance
Lightning Source LLC
La Vergne TN
LVHW080059070326
832902LV00014B/2310